Finding Hope

Life After Trauma

By Shekinah Shakti

Finding Hope: Life After Trauma

Written by Shekinah Shakti

Published by Creative Connex Inc.

Cover by Alise Fife

Photos by Christina Marie Intimate Portraits

ISBN: 978-1-7382257-8-1

Printed in Canada

First Edition

For more information contact Shekinah at shekinah_shakti@outlook.com

Connex
PUBLISHING

Dedication

My first book was dedicated to my mom. She is still the reason I share my story. She didn't use her voice during her life and near the end, the strokes she had robbed her of it. The voice she didn't use, taken from her.

By telling her story, I give it back.

But this book, while still inspired by her, is dedicated to my daughters. May my vulnerability show them that there is beauty in being seen.

And may they always feel safe to speak their truth.

To Cheyenna and Ciara, my heart walking free in the world.

Finding Hope

There is something in a human being that is hard to kill
It's called hope
As long as you have it, you can find your way out of the darkness.

Preface

There is a belief among the Indigenous that before our souls come to earth, we sit with the Creator and decide our fate. I love this idea, but what really hit me was the part where our souls would choose our mothers with the intention of bringing them healing.

My mom passed away two years ago now, but I hope this book helps her spirit heal.

Five years ago I left my marriage of 27 years and realized that I had, unknowingly, followed my mother's path. I had married and given myself away. I had followed the generations of my family.

Every day since has been devoted to changing history, and this book is part of that. What started as self-reflection turned into my first book, *Good Morning*. And this is my second, as I grow even stronger and learn to heal.

This is my own love story where, after a lifetime of pain, I get to find out what life looks like after trauma. Every day I discover more, and each chapter of this book is dedicated to what I learn through the different aspects of my healing.

Finding Peace documents my last trip home to visit my father in the hospital. It's my dedication to my mother, who passed away more than a year previously. And it's where I find forgiveness for my parents, and peace in loss.

Finding Me is dedicated to learning how to love myself when, five years ago, at the age of 46, I realized I never knew how. It's filled with self-revelations and growth.

Finding Love is dedicated to just that–finding healthy love after a lifetime of trauma and emotional abuse. It's my love story with my boyfriend Dale, and the revelations that helped me find love again.

Finding Life is dedicated to my new life and ambitions. I've learned that I am stronger than I ever imagined, and capable of doing amazing things.

This book is the story of how the newest version of me came to be. Over my 52 years on this planet, there have been many different incarnations, but this is the one I like the best. She knows who she is for the first time in her life, and she has big dreams, and the confidence (or craziness), to believe she can. And she is passionate about helping those who are still where she has been.

Mom

You who held me first in the cradle of your ribs
And now that you are gone, I still feel your embrace
It's in the soft breeze
The dance of a butterfly around me
A random song that's not random at all
You were the first to hold me
And you've never let me go
Even in your death, you linger around me
And I am glad

Finding Peace

I remember coming home from seeing my mom alive for the last time. I knew I'd never see her again.

She had suffered several strokes and could no longer communicate or walk. The right side of her body was useless. Witnessing someone so important to you in that much suffering broke my soul.

The way I left hadn't been the way I wanted it to be. My brother was severely stressed while dealing with so much, and he was supposed to be the one to drive me to the airport to return home. But he chose that morning to get angry with me, and I was already so vulnerable and struggling desperately to hold back the tears. The confrontation immediately had me sobbing.

It's not how I wanted to say goodbye to her.

But I got on the plane and never saw her again.

That trip was hard. Not only because my mom was suffering and it was devastating to witness, but because my dad had turned into a nightmare.

At the time, we were unaware that he was in the beginning stages of dementia. He was losing his wife and himself at the same time. He was angry. He was mean. He had no patience for my mom. He was abusive to my brother and me.

My mom couldn't handle watching him belittle and mistreat her kids, so the very first night I stayed there, I lay awake listening to her sobbing in the room next to mine while my dad tried to defend himself.

Those moments still haunt me.

Returning home meant confronting everything I had witnessed while with my parents—along with a lifetime of pain. It was that trip that made me realize how much my relationship with my dad continued to influence the way I saw men.

At the time, I had started a short and chaotic relationship with someone who, in the beginning, I had so much hope for. He checked off so much of my list. Attractive, assertive, spiritual. He showed fascination in everything I did. I did reiki on him. We did meditation together. I taught him moon rituals.

But as soon as I made the trip home, he shifted. He ghosted me during the most painful time of my life. I'm still baffled by his behaviour at the time. How could anyone treat another grieving human like he did?

But clearly, I attracted a mirror. I was hurting and so was he. I also attracted a belief I didn't know I had until that visit home.

During that trip, I realized how deeply my dad's unkindness throughout much of my life had affected me as an adult. His dismissiveness towards my feelings and needs had shaped a subconscious belief within me—that all men were unkind. This belief became a self-fulfilling prophecy, as I found myself attracting men who were just like my father.

Those were hard epiphanies to face. And I was so angry. Angry at my dad for how he treated my mom. For how he treated us. Angry with God for letting my beautiful mom hurt like that.

I don't remember ever feeling as mad as I did in those moments.

One night after arriving home, I purchased a bottle of rosé—my mom's favourite wine—and sat in the bath, crying and screaming at God. How could He let this happen?

I struggled with expressing my anger too. How could I be angry with my parents? My parents—who weren't perfect and who hurt me—but I also know loved me fiercely. I was raised to respect my parents. I was not allowed to be mad with them.

But I was.

I was mad that they had hurt me and that I had, in turn, passed on the generational trauma to my own children. I was angry that my relationship with my father had impacted my life so deeply and caused me so much pain in adulthood.

I had to face my anger.

The lesson resides in the pain. As hard as those days were, it was those realizations that changed my life. I credit those lessons with changing what I had been creating in my life up until that point.

My mom got her wings less than a month after I returned home. I will miss her forever. My dad is in long-term care now. He's 91.

My brother has reconciled with him and has moved home to be there for him. My brother is a strong man.

And I've forgiven my dad. He did the best he knew how when raising us. He did what he believed to be right. He did what was done to him.

I am now grateful for the lessons and for where they led me. I'm in a better place.

And now, I have a kind man in my life.

The following are my reflections during my first visit to my hometown after my mom's passing as I returned to see my dad now diagnosed with dementia and living in the hospital.

Today I will get on the plane to go to see my dad.

It's my first trip home since my mom passed away. I keep thinking about how it will feel to walk into their house and have her not be there.

But I am there to see my dad. My dad who's been living in the hospital for five months because there is no room for him in a long-term care facility. I have no idea how he will receive me. What will he remember? He may not even remember that I've left my marriage and have a new life.

Last time I was there, I was pretty mad at him. I was grieving for my mom, who would pass away just weeks after I left. My dad had been argumentative, and sometimes outright cruel during that visit.

When I returned home, I had a lifetime of childhood wounds to face—ones that I hadn't yet confronted.

Over the year since my mom passed away, I had tried to process my emotions about my dad and find a sense of peace. As a father, he did the best he knew how. At 89, he didn't understand he had hurt anyone. I know he certainly never intended to.

Then, in the spring, when his neighbours reached out to let us know my dad was not functioning well, and that he had been hospitalized and diagnosed with dementia, a lot of his behaviour from the last year began to make more sense.

His wife of 60 years was dying before his eyes, strangers were coming in and out of his home at all hours to take care of her, my brother—who had a complicated relationship with my dad— had moved in to help, and dementia was already taking away his mind. We didn't know, and neither did he.

So today, I am going home. Last year I went for my mom, and I was terrified to see her. Seeing her in pain was not something I wanted to do. But when it was over, I was so thankful for the time I had with her.

This time, I'm going back without the fear.

But I know I'm going to need some strength.

Last night, I slept where my mom used to sleep. I wasn't sure I would be able to bring myself to sleep in their bed, but when I got here, I decided I wanted to. I feel her here. I was talking to her last night as I went through her things. I know she is around me, even more now than when I was at home.

I found my parents' marriage license, along with some of her jewelry and toiletries—still here, like when she was. I found so many things I had given them over the years. There is so much of me in this house, too.

The moment I walked in the door, I started to cry. I put my hand on her urn. I found the malas I gave her last year in her jewelry box (one was for courage), and I'm wearing them now. I spent what felt like hours (I couldn't seem to stop) going through their things, until exhaustion won, and I crawled into their bed—on what would have been her side. And I cried.

But I am grateful to be here. There is a lot I want to do. I think this is good for me—to honour her. And for my dad. To help my brother. To help me move on.

Being here in my parents' home has deepened my faith. I've felt my mom's presence since the first night I arrived. I know she's here, surrounding me and my family.

When I first walked in the door, her prized Christmas cactus was still thriving, covered in blooms. It's a miracle, especially since she passed away over a year ago and hadn't been able to properly care for anything for a long time before her passing. No one else had watered or cared for the plant. Yet somehow it was still alive—and blooming.

As I looked through her closet, I had this overwhelming feeling that there was something my mom wanted me to find. I can't explain it. Just this knowing. But I was exhausted that night, so I went to bed and didn't look.

The next day, I told my brother about the feeling and mentioned that I thought it was Mom guiding me. He was dismissive, saying he had already searched the closet and there was nothing there. He was absolutely certain.

But as soon as I had time, I began to look through the closet. Immediately, I found something precious. I started laughing when I saw it.

It was something my brother, cousin, and sister had searched the entire house for and couldn't find. They were sure it was gone. It was a family heirloom of great value—my dad's giant Bible, which had been in our family for generations. It had been printed in 1895 and was filled with snippets from over the years—photos, obituaries, newspaper clippings, and even locks of hair from family who had passed away long ago.

I believe, without a doubt, that my mom guided me to it.

When I visited my dad at the hospital, there was a divider around his bed to offer some privacy. Throughout the room, there were many dividers, but my dad's was the only one with butterflies on it. Butterflies are a symbol of Mom for me, so much so that I even have a tattoo of a butterfly in her memory.

Last night, as I went through her things, I found a card with butterflies on it.

She is all the way around me here.

It's such a beautiful blessing.

Today was hard.

Today, my brother and I talked. We talked about the summer Mom passed, and how she was in so much pain. We talked about Dad, and how bad everything had gotten.

I think I had blocked some of it out. It's so incredibly hard to think about how much Mom suffered.

Today, I also spoke to my sister, and we talked about the past—things that were painful.

I was going through Mom's dresser and found an envelope. When I opened it, I discovered photos she had printed of Leila, her beautiful little dog. With the photos was a folder about dealing with grief, and a paper with a poem about loss and death.

I cried.

I had bought her that dog.

My mom was very lonely. I lived on the other side of Canada, and my brother and sister weren't nearby either. Her friends had passed away or were far away, and my dad—well, he slept most of the time.

She lost her sight and wasn't able to do the things she used to, things that kept her occupied. She couldn't read, or watch TV or crochet, or even go on Facebook. She loved Facebook because it helped her stay in contact with her family in Nova Scotia and her kids.

So, I bought her Leila, and that dog became the love of her life. I've never seen a dog more spoiled or loved. Mom was always talking to her, hand-feeding her, buying her the best food. Leila was everything to her.

When Leila suddenly and traumatically passed away, Mom was absolutely heartbroken.

I don't think she ever fully recovered when Leila eventually passed. Something changed in Mom when she lost that dog.

Even writing this brings me to tears. I hate how much my mom hurt before she passed.

Today, my brother and I are taking my dad out of the hospital for lunch at Boston Pizza. I won't lie to you, I'm a little nervous about taking him out. My brother takes him out often, but sometimes it's difficult getting Dad to go back to the hospital afterward.

My dad won't want to return. He'll get angry and upset, and won't understand why he has to go back. He's often threatened suicide. All he wants is to go home, and he doesn't understand why he can't.

But regardless, my brother still takes him out and brings him back. He's learned that Dad will simply forget, and that—even though there have been some very traumatic moments—once Dad returns to the hospital, everything is fine.

I don't want to hear my dad say he wants to die. I'm sorry he can't go home. My brother has gotten used to it, but I'm not sure I can.

Still, I know my dad deserves to do things he enjoys. He deserves to get out of the hospital. He deserves to live life.

And going to Boston Pizza is important because it's for Mom.

We took her there the summer of my last visit, less than a month before she passed away. Spaghetti was her favourite. So, I made a point to take her when I was there.

We had to bring her in a wheelchair because she couldn't walk. And she had to eat her spaghetti with her left hand because she'd lost use of her dominant hand. The strokes she had robbed her of so much. But she was happy!!!

And there was spaghetti EVERYWHERE—on her face, all around her in the wheelchair, and on the floor too. But I didn't care. She didn't care. No one cared. It's a good memory.

So today, we will go to Boston Pizza for Mom.

There are things I don't like to think about.

Like last year, when I came to my parents' home to see my mom before she passed. The night I arrived was rough.

My dad was being unkind to everyone, and my mom couldn't take it. She refused to take her medication, and my dad took her into their bedroom. She was so upset with him, and you could hear my dad trying to explain himself.

And her sobbing.

Mom didn't normally cry. This made it even more devastating.

She was so helpless then. Her speech was gone. She couldn't walk unassisted. She couldn't take a bath or even go to the bathroom on her own. The entire right side of her body was paralyzed.

Now, I'm lying in their bed, where she would have been.

It's so hard not to carry her pain.

\When I boarded the plane to return home after seeing my family during the summer of 2022, I knew I'd never see my mom again.

I was grief-stricken. Mad as hell. And all of the wounds of my childhood were ripped wide open.

I was so angry with my dad. And after spending years reconciling my past and working on healing, I was trying to process why I had become the woman I was.

I remember buying a bottle of wine, drinking it in the bathtub, crying and yelling at God. *Why did my beautiful mom have to hurt so much? Why?*

It was a few weeks later that my mom passed away. My brother texted me the news. Immediately I felt sick and retched over the toilet. I've never felt that feeling before. My whole world shattered. As much as I knew it was coming, and that her death was a kindness (no longer was she in pain), I will never get over not having her here.

I will never hear her voice again. Hear her call me Lovey. Or how she said my name with emphasis on the second "e"—"*Sherreeey*". I will miss her forever.

And I still had to deal with my anger towards my dad. My dad, who lost his wife of 60 years. At 88 years old, he was not okay himself.

But it didn't help that he seemed so ready to move on and find another wife. He took a bunch of Mom's things in to donate almost immediately.

I know my dad's mental state wasn't well, so I don't want his actions to be judged. I'm just trying to be transparent, and the truth isn't always pretty.

My brother had his own grief and anger, as did my sister, too. My sister was still recovering from her own battle with cancer at the time. Our family was devastated.

In the months that followed, my dad was all alone.

My brother, overwhelmed with anger, didn't even want to talk to him and was living several hours away. My sister was on Vancouver Island, and I was in Ontario. We were all grieving.

Even the phone calls with Dad were difficult, but I tried my best to understand. My dad was doing what he always did—the best he knew how. He was a hurt man.

I don't know everything about his childhood, as he rarely shared much. But I know enough to understand he carried wounds of his own, also given to him by his well-meaning parents.

We can only do what we know. Good old generational trauma.

My dad loved us the best he knew how.

Now he was alone. After being so dependent on my mom for 60 years. Looking back, I realize he was in the early stages of his dementia, which would have amplified it all.

In the months that followed, he had a lot of difficulty. The deep freezer filled with meat broke down, and the contents rotted, leaving the house filled with the stench of rotten meat. A bear even tried to break in to get at it.

His driving became so dangerous that his doctor reported him, and his car was towed home. He got sick from eating food that he didn't know wasn't safe to eat. He didn't know about food safety because he had my mom for that.

And then, he was put in the hospital.

That was a godsend. From so far away, feeling helpless, I finally felt that, hopefully, he was safe.

After he was hospitalized, all the remaining anger I held towards him left me. It's gone now. He tried his best and I know that.

What I do still carry is deep grief for my mom. Not because she's dead. I'm so grateful that she's not suffering anymore. But I'm still grieving how much pain she endured. Not just in those final months, but in her whole life.

That still hurts.

I don't know if I'll ever get over that.

And this is why I tell her story. Our story.

I've had a complicated relationship with my father. We haven't always seen eye to eye. I have fought with him. I have been angry with him. I have held bitterness and resentment towards him.

But at the end of the day he has always been there for me. And he has loved me the best way he knew how.

Watching him fade away with dementia has taken away any lingering anger or resentment. He is just a man who's always tried to do what he thought was right. He taught me integrity and honesty. He taught me to work hard and have pride in what I do. He taught me morality and ethics.

Many of the things I am today are because of him.

And for that I am grateful

So much of who I am was given to me by both my mom and my dad. Through their actions, I learned what I want to carry forward and what I do not. Sometimes, those lessons came from things they did that I've chosen not to follow.

But they were only human, doing the best they could.

Just as I am, doing the best I can.

I hope my children can give me the same grace.

One of the biggest gifts my parents gave me was guilt. It wasn't a gift I wanted.

I grew up in a household where in order to be loved, I believed I needed to be GOOD. Later conversations with my siblings and my mom helped me understand that they felt the same way. Though my dad never told me, I believe he too carried that wound as well.

I come from a family with strict religious beliefs. The message was clear: if you do anything wrong, you will go to hell.

So you try not to do anything wrong. You try to be perfect. And then when perfection isn't possible—or when you inevitably fuck up because you are only human—you feel like the worst person in the world.

When you begin your life like that, the guilt and shame start to pile on. Add to that the belief that you must martyr yourself for your family, and pretty soon you have made yourself responsible for everyone's happiness. And when (not if) you fail, carrying that guilt is heavy.

Even now, with all the awareness I have, I still carry that guilt. When I think about my mom and her final years, the guilt is overwhelming.

My mom was often lonely. I moved away, and so did my siblings. My dad wasn't always the greatest company. Even my mom's friends were eventually all gone. But from the other side of Canada, I tried my best to help her. There is solace in that. Walking into my mom's house reminds me of all I tried to do to help her. I sent mementos reminding her she was loved and not alone. There are angel necklaces and plaques, and even a pillow embroidered with "I love you, Mom."

For a while, my mom found Facebook as a new way to connect It was a blessing for her until her sight began to deteriorate. So I did my best to help her by purchasing a keyboard with giant numbers. Seeing it now in my parents' home is a reminder that I did try.

That is when I bought her Leila, her beloved dog. For a few precious years, Mom had company. But when Leila eventually passed away, my mom's heart was broken.

By that point, my own life was changing drastically. My 27-year marriage had ended. After years of being a stay-at-home-mom, I became a yoga instructor with a crazy busy schedule. I got my own apartment, and everything in my life was different. I was going out and enjoying life. I was actually living—I think for the first time ever.

I was focused on healing and finding happiness. But with those wonderful changes came financial constraints. I could no longer afford to send Mom things like I used to. Her life grew darker, and I wasn't there.

Those last years haunt me.

Her health continued to deteriorate. They found a tumour in her brain. Her vision was getting worse despite painful treatments every 6 weeks. She was on insulin and her blood sugar was never stable. Her kidneys were failing. She had arthritis and was in a lot of physical pain.

She was deeply depressed.

Then the pandemic happened, and my parents couldn't even go to the mall. I would phone them and could barely hear over the news blaring on their tv. It was a horrible time for all of us, but especially them. They lived in fear.

My mom would start to have a series of strokes, and that was the worst of all. I had no idea how bad it could get until then. Now Mom, fully aware of everything happening around her, was trapped in her body. The right side of her body paralyzed and her speech deeply impaired.

Even though my mom was still alive, I grieved for her. The distance between us meant all I had was phone calls with her, but I could no longer understand anything she said. Yet she would try so hard to talk. And if you had patience, you could tell she was clear about what she wanted to say—she just couldn't make the words come out.

If I can say anything about my mom, it's that she was the strongest human I have ever known. Even with her strokes, she didn't give up.

My dad had no patience for her at all. This was the worst time for their relationship. He upset her so badly, that one evening, even though she could barely walk, she packed herself a suitcase and was ready to leave.

When that happened, my dad called her crazy. That didn't help. My mom had a temper, and his words deeply upset her. She wasn't crazy. She was trapped in a body that was betraying her.

I'm grateful I was able to see her before she passed. That visit absolutely broke my heart, and I will never get over seeing her in so much pain. But I also got to help her take a bath and paint her nails. She got to give my daughters and I gifts. We FaceTimed my daughter and drank rosé with her. I played her old songs from childhood and we just spent time together. We both knew I'd never see her again. We both knew she was dying.

At least I can find comfort in knowing she left this world certain of how deeply I love her.

And that's all I have, because this wasn't something I had in my power to fix—no matter how "good" I was.

I threw up last night. I'm not sure why. I don't normally throw up, but since coming home, I have had lots of tummy trouble—which leads me to my morning thoughts.

Yesterday, I wrote about my need to be the "good" kid. That's truly defined my whole life, and if I'm being honest with myself, that aspect of me has not really changed. I still want to be seen as "good" in everything I do.

I came to my parents' home with thoughts of grandeur. My brother has been taking care of everything here alone and has faced many struggles. I wanted to come home and fix it all.

But I can't.

I can't fix everything. The first few days, I pushed myself hard, trying to clean and organize my mom's bedroom. We were going to bring some things to the thrift store and divide sentimental items among the family. I thought I'd start in their bedroom and work my way through the whole house.

I took on too much.

Nothing is final yet. We can't sell the house, and there is no urgency to do it all immediately. So, after those hectic first few days, I slowed myself down.

Every day, we visit my dad in the hospital. You never know what you are going to get when you see him.

Yesterday, he was a reminder of his worst self. Honestly, overall, my dad is much better now. He's happy to see us and has a childlike quality. He can be confused at times, but he's not mean. I do think he can be a handful for the caregivers at the hospital, and can be difficult or even confrontational, but my experience with him has been good overall.

But yesterday, I was reminded of why I used to be so angry with him. He put down my brother and accused me of lying. It wouldn't have mattered if this was just behaviour connected to his illness, but it was more than that. It was an echo of who he used to be.

It was a trigger, and it brought me back.

I used to visit my parents every summer with my kids. I'm so thankful for those memories, and I am grateful my daughters had a wonderful relationship with their grandparents. Where I never knew my grandparents, they were close to theirs. That is something I am so proud of.

But those visits would fill me with anxiety. It was my job to fairly divide time between the relatives, because early on it caused problems. It was my duty to keep everyone happy. I always had tummy issues during these visits.

Just like now.

My boyfriend sent me this quote this morning,

"Control what you can, give all you can. If the result isn't what you'd hoped for you can be proud of the effort and reflect in a way you can learn, rather than regret."

I do. I always give all I can. I just have to remember to let go of what I can't change. And to know that I've always done all I could.

My mom had a complicated relationship with her mother.

She held many resentments towards my grandmother's choices during her childhood. She judged her mother harshly.

When she married my dad and they left Nova Scotia to create a life in British Columbia, I think part of it was her attempt to leave behind her mother and that chapter of her life.

I remember when my grandmother passed away. We were on a camping trip, like so many times before. This was well before cell phones existed, so there was no way to contact us.

On our way back home, my mom had a horrible headache and an overwhelming feeling of dread. She didn't want to go home, and she didn't know why. She just knew something was wrong.

My mom was gifted with a strong intuition. There were many times growing up that she just knew things.

This time was no exception, and it has stayed in my memory.

When we returned home, we found out that my mom's family in Nova Scotia had been trying to reach us to let us know my grandmother was dead. It was a sudden and unexpected death.

I was small at the time, and too young to understand. But now that I've lost my own mom, I feel for what she must have gone through.

She was not able to go home to grieve her mother. At the time, she still held such complicated feelings towards her. She would later tell me the full story of why she had such anger towards her mother and tell me that she had reconciled those feelings. But, by that time, it was too late to tell her.

This is what she told me:

My grandmother's life was hard. She got pregnant young, and in those days, you were forced to get married when that happened. So, regardless of the fact that my grandparents made a horrible couple, they were wed. They went on to have 9 children.

My grandfather wasn't very reliable. He was known to disappear and leave my grandmother and the children to fend for themselves. This wasn't a time when women worked, so this left my grandmother with the predicament of how to feed her kids. She was terrified that her children would be taken from her.

My mom believed that my grandmother invited men into the home to exchange sex for money. This disgusted my mom, and she held this against her mother until it was too late, and my grandmother was gone.

Over time, years after my grandmother's passing, she would find compassion for the woman who had done everything she could to keep her family together.

Personally, I see my grandmother as an incredibly strong woman.

I have something with my mom that she never had with hers: time. And I'm so grateful for that. It also matters so deeply to me that my mom passed away knowing I loved her.

I'm sure she wished she could have given the same to her mother.

If you are holding on to the past—resentments, anger, or regrets—I urge you to try to reconcile them as best you can, while you can. As humans, we are only capable of doing the best we know how.

And sometimes, we don't know how at all.

I put up my mom's Christmas tree today.

My mom was pretty depressed the last Christmas she was alive. I'm not sure she even bothered to put the tree up.

My brother was having car trouble and couldn't make the trip home that year. It was still during the pandemic, and she just wasn't feeling it.

It wasn't the first Christmas she didn't want to put the tree up. But even from the other side of Canada, I was usually pretty good at convincing her to do it anyway.

Christmas was hard for her after we all left—my brother, sister and me. We all moved away. I moved to Ontario, and I never spent another Christmas with her after that. That was 29 years ago.

Now, my dad is in the hospital and my brother is staying in my parents' home. And I felt like this place still needed some joy in it.

So, my brother helped me dig out her tree and ornaments, and I put them up in the window facing the road—so that people driving by can see her lights.

She may be gone, but her light is still here

Miss you, Momma.

Dementia.

My dad is currently in the hospital, staying on the first floor in a ward ironically called "short-term stay," though his stay there may be as long as two years. There simply isn't enough room for all the elderly in need of long-term care.

He doesn't have a room. The ward is full, and all the rooms are taken, so he's been given a bed placed in the dining room. His bed isn't the only one there. Beds line the walls of the room.

Since I have been visiting my dad, I've gotten to know a few of his neighbours.

There is Edith—an absolutely beautiful woman with stunning blue eyes. Generally speaking she is irritable and not to be messed with.

Then there is Wanda. She likes to talk. *A lot*. Today, she was painting her nails a burgundy colour and was very pleased when I told her they were pretty.

And there is a woman my dad calls Gurdy. Gurdy was a real person my dad knew growing up in Nova Scotia, and even though this woman can't possibly be her, he thinks it is. My dad likes her a lot and has been talking about deciding to date her—whether she gets a say in the matter seems debatable. She knows me by name now and always says hello.

All of them seem to have different degrees of needs. Some seem worse than my dad. Others seem pretty normal.

Including this one woman who likes to keep active by walking around the ward. I think she's beautiful, and she seemed relatively normal to me. When my very flirty father asked her for a hug, she and I shared a smile that seemed to tell me she was aware. There goes my dad again.

But when I went to bring my dad back to the ward tonight, I walked in to find her with company. As she saw me, she excitedly introduced me to someone she called her sister. Only thing was that the woman she thought was her sister was really her daughter. Her daughter's eyes connected with mine and I silently sent her my sympathy.

Fuck dementia.

If my mom was still alive, today would have been my parents' 62nd wedding anniversary.

My parents met in Nova Scotia. From the stories my mom told me, my dad was well known in the community for being a "ladies' man." At first, she wanted no part of him.

But he pursued her, and she eventually gave in. After two months of dating (or "courting," as my dad would call it), my parents were wed. It was a simple wedding—just my parents and another couple as witnesses. My mom wore a green dress, her favourite colour.

They would move into my dad's family farm. Both his parents had passed, and his siblings moved away, leaving him to run the farm alone. I don't know a lot about those early days, except that there was a young boy in the neighbourhood my mom had taken in. He had a developmental disability and was neglected. Mom had a nurturing nature, so she cared for him. I don't know his real name, but she called him Sambo. When my dad decided to sell the farm and join his brother in BC, Sambo was left behind. This broke my mom's heart. She never forgot Sambo, and she always wondered if he was okay.

They sold everything that didn't fit in their car and drove across Canada to a new life.

They had many struggles. Financially it was pretty rough. But if there was a will there was a way, and eventually they would build a home on Chief Lake Road beside my dad's brother's home.

My mom wanted a family more than anything, and they kept trying to get pregnant. Getting pregnant wasn't the problem though, it was staying pregnant. My mom endured multiple miscarriages.

Years later, I myself had one miscarriage. At the time, it made me wonder how my mom survived having so many. My miscarriage devastated me, and I already had a healthy baby when I endured it. My mom dreamed of becoming a mother, but that dream kept being taken from her.

Eventually, after several miscarriages, my parents decided to adopt, and my brother joined the family. Soon after the decision to adopt, my mom became pregnant with my sister. And five years later, I was their final surprise.

My mom had one more miscarriage after me and it almost killed her. She hemorrhaged badly, and after that, the doctor tied her tubes.

But my mom had her family.

My parents were a traditional, old-fashioned couple. My dad worked in forestry, and my mom was a stay-at-home-mom. Neither of them followed their dreams. My dad should have been a carpenter. He was so skilled with woodworking. My mom always wanted to be a hairdresser.

But those things weren't in the cards for them.

Every once in a while, my mom would let us skip school so we could spend the day together and we'd go to the mall. I loved those days.

There were countless camping trips. I went fishing with my dad and brother and talked non-stop until my brother wanted to throw me overboard.

My sister and I loved to sing—so did my mom, actually. Music is a huge part of my memories. There are so many songs that take me back.

My dad would call my mom "Audi", instead of Audrey, and my mom would call my dad "Sugarbabe".

My parents had a very complicated relationship. I remember feeling frustrated about how my dad treated my mom.

But, without question, they loved us. And, without question, they loved each other in their broken way, but in the best way they knew how. We are all incapable of doing anything other than what we know.

So, please note that anything negative I say about them is still with love, but also with honesty. We cannot change what we don't know. I speak my family's truth so that future generations can do differently.

The very last anniversary my parents celebrated together was their 60th, and they drove to the other side of town to dine at their favourite restaurant. They ordered a bottle of wine to celebrate. Only problem was that my dad drank too much, and my mom was legally blind and unable to drive home. My 80-something-year-old parents had to cab it home that night because they had partied too hard. At the time, it made me laugh.

I can say many things about my family, both good and bad, but ultimately I can tell you that they loved us.

And that was the most important thing.

We decided not to tell Dad that today is his anniversary. Without being reminded, he wouldn't remember on his own, and we didn't want my dad to be sad.

Today is a reminder of everything that is gone.

But we also wanted to celebrate with him. Celebrate the 60 years my parents shared. The good. The bad. And the ugly.

So my brother and I decided to take him out to lunch. To Joey's Restaurant, a place that held many memories in my family.

It was the last place I ate with my parents before my life changed forever. I was nine months pregnant, and it would be the last time I would eat before going into labour with my first daughter. My parents would jokingly say I had my "last meal" there.

My dad once had a heart attack at that restaurant and we had to rush to the emergency. My daughters were with us. It was a terrifying day, and one I'll never forget.

We had also been there many other times that were absolutely uneventful.

My brother has his own memories there. He remembers going there after my mom had her strokes, and her attempting to eat with her left hand as her dominant hand was useless.

The walls of that restaurant had witnessed many cycles in our family's life.

So it made sense to go there in this new cycle. Without mom. But with her still in our hearts.

We ordered Dad his fish and chips and then ordered him a dessert. He deserved to celebrate, even if he didn't know he was.

And there was a moment when his cheesecake arrived— he remembered. He remembered being there years before with Mom, ordering cheesecake to celebrate their anniversary.

A magical moment.

And another one I won't forget.

Tomorrow morning I will get on a plane to go back home.

So today, I'm very reflective. It is 3:24 a.m. but I am awake, and my brain is full.

I'm lying in my parents' bed. I've been sleeping in their bed since I arrived here two weeks ago. When I got here, I didn't know if I could do that. I didn't know where I would sleep. Maybe on the couch, like I did last time I was here and my mom wasn't well.

While I was here last time, there was a lot of pain in this room. I heard my mom sobbing in here. I heard my parents fighting in here. My brother stayed with my parents for months while my mom's health declined, and he saw much more than I did. He will barely enter this room. He says the memories are too bad.

But as soon as I walked in these doors, I felt Mom. Yes, I've slept in their bed, but exclusively curled on her side of the bed. I'm with her.

As you can tell, I was close to my mom. But I think I would be doing her a disservice to not acknowledge that she wasn't perfect. She made mistakes—many of which I found myself repeating as a mother.

We can only do what we know.

She did what she knew.

She used guilt and shame as punishment. She was the Queen of the silent treatment. She treated us more as friends than her children and told me about her grievances against my dad. I grew up wanting to protect my mom from my inconsiderate father. No child should ever feel like that. And despite that, she always took my dad's side, even when he was hurtful and wrong.

Me too.

I followed in her footsteps. With my own kids, I did many of the same things. I put myself last, just as she did. I mirrored her in so many ways.

It's taken me a while to forgive myself. I have shed so many tears over my own mistakes.

But, when it comes to my mom, I think I've always forgiven her. I have never been angry with her. She made mistakes as a mother, she put me in the position to feel like I needed to protect her and stand up for her, but regardless, I'm so grateful for how close that made us. We talked about EVERYTHING—including, in the later years, her regrets.

There were many things she wished she could have done differently. I don't think she believed she was a good mom and, that broke her heart because being a mom was the single most important thing to her.

I told her that she was a wonderful mom, and I meant it. I will never be loved again as much as she loved me. And she inspired me with her strength and resilience.

But the greatest lessons she gave me came from her mistakes. There are many things I will do differently because of what she taught me.

And as much as I have admired her strength, I actually think that is still very toxic. No one should be admired by how much pain they can endure. It still haunts me how much she went through.

But part of my healing here is to remember that, as much as I put myself in the role of her protector, that was never supposed to be my job. The life she had was her choosing, and I was never responsible for her happiness.

It still hurts. I still would have loved to save her

Love you forever, Momma.

Today is my last day here, and I've been reflecting on so much. I feel like I'm going home as a different person. A lot of my reflection was about my family's pain, but it certainly wasn't all bad.

I was so blessed to have them.

And I truly hope that when I leave this world, my kids will remember the good, not just the bad.

So here's some good.

My mom sang all the time. I listen to so much music, and it all reminds me of her. Willie Nelson, Johnny Cash, Loretta Lyn, Hank Snow, Randy Travis. The list is long, and such a gift.

She loved Elvis—he was her childhood crush. My dad, naturally, wasn't so fond of him because of that.

She loved to feed us, and I have wonderful memories of her food. Date squares, homemade donuts, beans, and chicken stew. But my greatest memory is coming home to the house filled with the smell of fresh bread. To this day the smell of bread means her.

When I was little, I remember her and I cuddling on the couch. She would always rub my back, and it made me feel safe.

We watched *The Young and the Restless,* that crazy soap opera. When my girls were old enough, they would also watch with her.

My dad worked hard, always. When he was home, he was always doing something. When he was older and had many ailments, he'd still be busy. Mom would say he was always getting in trouble because he would often do too much, and ultimately be in pain after.

He was an amazing artist with wood. I'm taking home some of the things he made. Those too are a gift.

My parents always celebrated every birthday. There was always the "Happy Birthday" song and cake. When I moved away, my mom would phone to make sure to sing it to us.

Holidays mattered, and Christmas was magical when I was little.

Lunch was at 12:00 and dinner at 5:30. Always. And we ate at the table together.

My parents took us on endless trips. We drove across Canada when I was six. I've been to Vancouver, Jasper, Vancouver Island, Edmonton, and Calgary countless times. I've been fishing and hiking. I grew up playing by the campfire and eating my own roasted hotdogs.

Our lives were full. And we loved one another.

Were we perfect? Hell no. But I was still blessed.

Thank you, Mom and Dad. I will love you forever.
It's my last night here, in the city I was raised in.
I've been here for two weeks, and it feels like I've been here forever. But at the same time, it went by fast.

The first week, I cried a lot. It was difficult. I found myself facing grief and guilt from my mom's passing which I didn't know still lived in me.

Seeing my dad, while still difficult, paled in comparison to dealing with the grief I have for my mom.

The second week there were less tears, but I do think that it was finally sinking in that my dad is truly losing himself. And it wasn't just my dad. It was getting to know the other people in my dad's ward.

Here are all of these beautiful people who used to have families and jobs and dreams and things they loved to do. All of that is gone. And they don't even know what happened.

I had a hard time not crying tonight when I left my dad for the last time.

This is the last night in my parents' bed, and lying where my mom once rested is difficult because it reminds me of how everything has changed.

Change always comes. In fact, every time I would come for a visit, when I left, I knew it would not be the same when I returned.

It's no different this time.

When I come back again, things will be different.

It makes me ache for the past. For happier times.

For Mom….

I'm here at the airport now. The same airport my mom and dad brought me to many times over. I'm so grateful for the countless trips I was able to make with my daughters as they grew. I'm grateful that they got to love their grandparents.

But the end of those visits were always difficult. I hated saying goodbye, and Mom would always cry.

Today, as my brother drove me here, the sky was shining so beautifully—the sun rising on this day. And on the way up, there was even a bear on the cliff we drove past. Spiritually, bears represent courage, and they've been around me a lot on this trip home.

My brother and I talked about the day I left the last time I was here. When my mom was so sick.

We were all struggling on that day. My brother was a volcano waiting to blow. That morning, he blew up on me. I was trying so hard to be strong for my mom but I also knew it was the last time I'd ever see her. My brother's outburst made all my attempts fail and I dissolved into tears. I cried uncontrollably as I said goodbye.

I didn't want my final moments with her to be like that.

My brother regrets that day too.

But as we drove and talked about the mom that we both loved so much, and that in turn loved us as well, I couldn't help but think she was in that sunshine, and she had sent us that bear.

I think her message was that she's okay….

And for us to be brave.

I'm trying Mom.

Going back to my parent's home offered me an opportunity to face some important parts of myself in order to release some things that I have been carrying.

It is what we carry from the past that prevents us from moving forward in the future.

I've been carrying a lot. Grief and guilt over my mom's passing, and all that she went through. Releasing anger and judgment towards my dad. Forgiving people who I felt betrayed me. And surrendering to my faith.

I think this trip to my hometown helped me release it all.

Now that I've returned back to where I live, I'm back to facing some ongoing uncertainty about my future. I think I asked for it. I prayed for the universe to show me where He wanted me to be. I surrendered and God said, "Let's move you."

But all of this has sparked inspiration within me. It lit a fire in me. I've let go of fear. No matter what happens, I believe there is a plan for me, and that I am strong enough to face what comes.

I'm ready.

For My Daughters

Behind me stand the women of my origin

Women whose lessons were hard and unkind

Women who believed sacrifice was their gift

In their pain, I receive wisdom

Wisdom of generations

Wisdom for things I will no longer repeat

Sacrifice was their gift

And so is mine

For my daughters

Finding Me

Yesterday I Hated You

Yesterday I thought if I hated you enough you would be better

I starved you

Put your needs aside.

Chose others over you.

Looked at you in the mirror and criticized every detail, every scar, every roll, every flaw

I called you stupid

Told you you couldn't do anything right

Be better! Prettier, skinnier, smarter, sexier

Be a better mom, wife, daughter, friend, lover, person

Be better.

No, be perfect.

Perfect equals love

Yesterday I believed I could hate you perfect

But hate never made you perfect.

Hate made you sad.

Lost.

Alone.

Today I'm trying love instead

So I'm loving you

I'm nourishing you.

I'm putting you first.

I'm choosing you over everyone

I'm looking in the mirror and accepting you the way you are

And it's healing you

Making you better

When I was 19, I married my high school sweetheart, and I thought I had figured out life. At 19, I believed I knew everything. Now, at 52, I realize that I didn't know anything back then, and I still have a lot to learn.

We got married and had two beautiful daughters. Looking back, I understand now that we were both too young and broken to know what we were doing. Without skills like healthy communication, we struggled right from the beginning of our relationship.

Looking back, I can see it all.

You can only do what you know. All I knew came from my own family. I sacrificed myself. I used the skills my parents gave me, like guilt, manipulation, and the silent treatment. I hurt my ex. I hurt my kids. And I hurt myself.

27 years later I would leave the marriage and start the journey to heal from a lifetime of trauma, emotional abuse, and self-hatred. I spent my life trying to be what everyone else wanted, so after leaving my marriage, I had to learn who I was.

Five years have passed since I jumped into the unknown, and for the first time in my life, made a decision for myself. Over these past five years, I have had to overcome a lifetime of self-loathing, guilt, shame, and judgement. I have had to face the ugly parts of myself and find love for them. I have had to learn how to forgive myself, with the understanding that I could only do what I knew.

If someone asks you for an apple and all you have is an orange, that is all you have to give. All I had was what my parents taught me, and I didn't know I was doing wrong.

I've come a long way, but I still have a long way to go.

I have learned that the journey to finding self-love is just that: a journey, not a destination.

Because of the work I have done on myself, I now have more than an orange to give.

I now have the whole damn garden.

"Finding Me" is a reflection on my ongoing journey to self-love.

The person I was five years ago doesn't exist anymore. Neither does the girl I was a year ago. And definitely who I was ten years ago.

They are gone.

Never to return.

And I don't grieve for them. I have no grief for them—I have compassion for them. Being an over-thinker, I've analyzed their choices and made peace with their mistakes.

The versions of me from the past have made their mistakes.

But lately, I feel like I have reached a new level. There is a stark contrast between who I am now, and who I have been.

Usually with great inner change comes great outer change.

I'm excited to see what is coming.

But to quote a poem that resonates deeply:

"If you see the girl I used to be, thank her. We went through some hard shit together and she never left my side." ~Stephanie Bennet Henry.

I haven't written about this before, mostly because it involves my kids, and protecting their privacy matters to me. But I've alluded to the guilt I carry from their childhood, and I believe it's important to be open.

I hope my story helps you understand yours.

Regardless, I will be careful to avoid speaking to details that belong to my children. This is about me, not them.

I met their dad when I was 17. He was my first real boyfriend, and I fell hard. At 18, after graduating high school, we got our first apartment. At 19, we were married. And at 22—three years later—I gave birth to my first child.

I was an immature 22-year-old-woman. I had intentionally gotten pregnant because I thought I wouldn't ever feel lonely again if I had a baby. After all, a baby would love me.

The pregnancy wasn't what I expected. I had seen other pregnant women who were adorable. I wasn't cute. I had acne all over my face and back. My feet and ankles swelled. Bright red stripes covered my stomach—yes, those beloved stretch marks, giving me another reason to believe myself ugly. Despite not gaining much weight, I was huge. Everything hurt. Pregnancy wasn't fun.

The labour was terrifying. Despite faithfully reading What to Expect when You are Expecting, I wasn't ready. I don't think anyone can prepare you for that pain.

But she was born.

I swear I had PTSD after her delivery. I couldn't stop talking about the labour. It was a story stuck on repeat in my head. My perineum tore despite the doctor performing an episiotomy. I had no muscle control down there, and going to the bathroom was an adventure. I couldn't hold anything.

But she was born.

No one can explain to you what it feels like to be a mother. The closest description I can give is that it's as if someone reached into your chest, tore out your heart, and set it free. The love I immediately felt for her was all-encompassing. A literal piece of me was free in the world, and it was both the most beautiful and the most terrifying thing. I had to keep her safe! And she felt so vulnerable.

At the time, her dad and I were living with his parents. Only weeks after her birth, they would kick us out. It was a very unstable time for us. We ended up moving in with one of her dad's friends.

I believe the sadness and stress I felt during that time went into her. She was very attached to me. I couldn't leave her without her crying nonstop until I returned. And she ended up with colic, which meant she would cry every single day inconsolably for hours.

I got used to it. I let myself go and sacrificed everything for her. It surprised me. I was so young and immature at the time, and I didn't understand what it meant to be a mother. My life wasn't mine anymore.

It was hers.

I think I grieved that—the loss of me.

Three years and nine days later, I brought my second daughter into the world. She was entirely different. The labour wasn't hard. I wasn't terrified this time, and she came quickly. She looked exactly like her sister. But that's where the similarities ended.

She was a delight! An easy baby.

Looking back, I know I was still not okay. I had postpartum depression but was never diagnosed. I was a walking shell. I'm not sure if the veil of sadness ever lifted. When I think about it, I realize that sadness began even before either of them were born.

By the time my second daughter arrived, we had moved out of our hometown and were living in Vancouver. Shortly after her birth, her dad was offered a promotion that required us to move across Canada.

When my oldest was three years old and my youngest seven months, we moved.

At the time, I was convinced their dad was cheating on me. I'm not sure if he was—I know I'll never know the truth, and it doesn't matter now. But I was broken and completely alone. Moving meant I was now far away from my family and friends.

All I had were my two girls.

My husband, my girls, and I moved away—far away from my parents and friends. At least when we were living in Vancouver, our families could still drive down every once in a while. But Toronto was too far.

I was alone with two small kids.

Their dad left early in the morning and was gone until late evening. Despite the loneliness, I figured it out and got used to life being just me and those two girls.

We lived in Mississauga for six years. The apartment we lived in was in a lower-income area where many immigrants came to Canada to start a new life. My girls were the only white kids in their class at school and were given a sort of celebrity status because they were different. Both of them were beautiful kids. My oldest looked like Rapunzel, with blonde curls down to her butt. My youngest has these enormous blue eyes that she quickly learned to use as a tool. All she had to do was bat her big blue eyes and she could get anything she wanted.

When my kids were six and nine years old, we bought our first home together. It was a two-hour drive from my husband's work, meaning long commutes for him and even longer days spent alone with the kids for me. But by then, that felt normal.

Our new home was in a predominantly white city, and the girls were no longer treated as special. My oldest began to struggle with bullying while my youngest made friends easily.

Looking back, I can see now how this was a pattern. Even as babies, my oldest struggled while my youngest seemed to have it easier.

I began to focus on my oldest. The hardest thing as a parent is seeing your child hurt, but my attempts didn't seem to help. Her teachers weren't receptive. I think pretty early on, I became a helicopter mom, trying to protect her.

Their father was gone for work a lot, and when he was home, he was often cranky and hard on them. I walked on eggshells around him as well and didn't stand up for them. I was meek and afraid to speak up against him.

For my kids, there were two dynamics in our house: their strict and rigid father, and their mother, who was a child like them. I was scared of their dad and I acted like a kid, not the adult I was supposed to be. I look back on that with regret. I also realize that I wanted to be my daughters' friend. So I often played the role of friend, not mother.

Looking back, I have to acknowledge I played the role of the "good" parent with them. Their dad was mean and I was nice. Subconsciously, I liked that role. It's not something that I am proud of now, but I'm being honest. This dynamic mirrored my own childhood.

I was put in the same position with my older sister. She was always getting in trouble with my parents, and I was always the "good" kid. It's a role that felt comfortable, and I jumped into it. After all, all I ever wanted was to be loved. When my sister was criticized and I was given approval, it fed my need to be "good."

I wanted my kids to love me. I had them with the hope of finding that love. I believed that having children would mean always having someone who loved me.

I was love-starved.

So from the get-go, our family was broken and odd.

The high school years with my kids were even more complicated. My oldest struggled with panic attacks, depression, and self-harm. I hovered more, trying to help. I took her to the family doctor, but he was dismissive, and I didn't know what else to do.

So I hovered. We grew very close.

My youngest was a regular teenager who knew how to push my buttons. We fought, and a wall began building between us. I had no emotional intelligence or any clue how to regulate my emotions, so I made mistakes.

She was struggling with her own anxiety and life problems, and I couldn't see it. She was good at masking and pretending she was okay, but while I was busy hovering over her sister, she needed me and I wasn't there.

My husband and I were falling apart. I was deeply depressed. I would get up in the morning to get everyone else ready for school and work, pretending I was okay, but as soon as everyone left, I crawled back into bed. I had suicidal thoughts. Life was dark, and I was barely hanging on.

How could I take care of them when I couldn't even take care of myself?

A series of difficult events began to unfold one after another. My husband's father got sick with cancer and passed away. My husband had a serious car accident. He lost his job. All while he and I continued to fall apart.

The loss of my husband's job pushed us both into the next chapter of my family's life. We both went back to school and started new careers.

I became a yoga instructor.

That decision changed everything. I believe it was the spark that helped me find the courage to leave my marriage and start the life I have now.

But I made mistakes. The ones I regret the most are the ones that hurt my kids.

My youngest and I are healing now, having open conversations about the past.

I haven't seen my oldest in almost a year now. I miss her every day. But I trust in her wisdom, and I believe in her. Regardless of whether she chooses to have me in her life, I send her my love every single day.

To this day, she is still my heart walking free in this world.

Last spring, my youngest daughter ended an engagement and an eight-year relationship. Watching your kid go through pain is hard. You don't want them to hurt.

But I also know this is part of her journey, and the last thing I want is for her to follow in her parents' footsteps. She isn't. She's seeing things that I didn't and choosing differently.

I'm proud of her.

I know she is still grieving. It's hard to let go of the future you once envisioned.

When I left her dad, I was 20 years older than she is now. I had stayed in that relationship for years, despite being unhappy and knowing I should leave. If I'm honest with myself, probably over 10 years.

That sounds crazy right? Looking back, it wasn't fair to anyone, but I did it in the name of "doing the right thing."

It's what our parents did. My parents were together for 60 years before my mom passed.

I remember listening to my daughter talk about her best friend's parents—how their split caused so much messiness, betrayal, and hurt. My daughter could not understand why those parents would do that to their kids.

Little did she know, I too wanted to leave her dad, but those conversations made me stay. I stayed for her.

That was one of the reasons why I stayed. I also stayed because I was financially dependent on him and getting older, and convinced no one else would love me. Most of all, I was afraid of being alone forever.

So I stayed. I stayed and I was angry. The longer I stayed, the more I blamed him. Made him the villain.

I hurt him because I stayed. Yet I believed I was also staying for him. Despite my anger, I didn't want to hurt him.

Two opposites can exist at the same time. You can be angry with someone and also care about them. I was furious with him, but also wanted him to be okay. And I knew he wasn't. Neither of us were.

Looking back, my decision to stay hurt him—hurt me and my kids. If I could go back in time, I would have left. But we can't go back, and all things happen as they were meant to.

I know this.

By the time I left, the grief for our marriage was gone. Yes, I grieved for what I thought my future was going to be. I grieved the family and the kids. But I didn't grieve him.

The anger destroyed us. That is sad to admit.

I know my daughter still grieves for her ex. In those eight years, he became part of our family, so I miss him too. And wish him well.

I don't write about my life to paint anyone as a villain. My ex is not a bad person. He's actually kind and intelligent and funny. He tries really hard in everything he does. I wish him love and happiness.

But he hurt me. And I hurt him too. We hurt each other.

Now I understand us better. When we met as kids we were already hurting. Our family traumas matched, and we already knew how to dance in our toxic ways from the get-go.

He was my mirror. His family dynamic was the same as mine. He, too, came from generations of codependent and narcissistic relationships.

We knew exactly how to fall into the patterns of the past.

But there are no villains and no victims here. Just broken people doing what they know.

If you want different, you must do different.

Gratefully, the world is beginning to understand family trauma and is working to change it. Although, I still hear it presented in a way that makes someone out to be the bad guy. The word "narcissist" gets used freely and is often blanketed towards the man in a relationship.

But the truth I've learned is that if you are a product of emotional abuse, chances are you have narcissistic tendencies. And they come in totally different degrees, depending on your own fears.

Did my ex have narcissistic tendencies? Yes. That is why, at first, he was the villain in my story—why I justified my anger towards him.

But here's the thing—when I left him and had to look in the mirror, I discovered I had some of those tendencies too.

When I first learned about the codependent/narcissistic relationship, there was one aspect that stood out to me, and made the decision to leave final: I learned that narcissistic people are incapable of ever healing. Incapable. It's impossible.

As soon as I heard this, I was leaving.

However, I now realize it is more complex than this. If you have narcissistic traits, you can still heal. I'm proof of this. I believe now narcissism has different degrees and for most of us, healing is still possible.

I lived years in my "he was the villain" story, filled to the brim with anger. It was impacting my health. It hurt my family. Now, I see it all so differently. I see my own role, and I know I was to blame too.

And I hope that my mistakes will help my daughters. I think they already are.

In the months after leaving my marriage, I was hurting and scared, and filled with self-loathing. But believe it or not, I'm now grateful for what I went through. All of it. I look at the woman I once was with pride. Yes, I was messy, and I made so many mistakes. I drank to try to escape the pain, and that just made everything worse.

But I was healing for the first time in my life.

I had always hated myself. My parents were well-meaning but emotionally abusive and they taught me I was never good enough.

I used to think emotional abuse was someone calling you names and putting you down. I have since learned that I have experienced it my whole life. Emotional abuse looks like guilt. Manipulation. Gaslighting. And my mom's favourite, the silent treatment.

I was raped at 14. At the time I was so innocent and naive. I was still a virgin, and I had this idea that only someone who loved me would take that from me. It really messed me up, and I don't think I ever healed from it. It happened on a Friday, and by Monday, I was at school like it never happened. I pushed it down and life went on.

At 19 I married my husband, who was my first, but he was emotionally abusive too. We both were. I stayed with him for 27 years, and by the time I left, I was a shell of a human.

Leaving him was the beginning of my healing journey, and that, in itself, has been a hell of a journey.

And yet, I am still thankful. For everything. Because the woman you know now would have never existed without what I've been through. And because (not despite) my pain, I'm so passionate about helping other people. It's made me who I am, and for the first time in my whole life, I am proud of myself.

We are made up of our life experiences, and that includes the pain. I would say it's the pain we endure that shapes us most of all.

So yes, I'm willing to say that I'm grateful for my trauma. It was all a gift because it brought me here.

And I love where I am now.

When I was 3 years old, the family dog was hit and killed by a car in front of me.

I was playing in the front yard, and the neighbour's dog had crossed the street into our yard. Our dog had chased him back onto his property but hadn't seen the car coming. My parents said he was protecting me.

It was my fault.

Afterwards, the whole family stood together in the kitchen, crying. My dad. My mom. My sister. My brother. I remember going from one person to the other, trying to make it better. Trying to fix it.

I was in a panic, terrified. I had never seen my parents cry before. If my parents were crying, then it must be very, very bad.

It's one of my earliest memories, and looking back, I believe that experience formed the woman I was to become.

I have always taken on the responsibility of other people's wellness, to my own detriment. I have had to face the guilt I carry for things that aren't in my control—like my mom's loneliness and unhappiness.

It's crazy to realize I started carrying the weight of my family when I was 3 years old.

Even then, believing it was all my fault.

Sacrificing yourself for the people you love doesn't make you a good person. Let me say it louder for those in the back: giving yourself away, saying yes to things that you don't want to do, and exhausting yourself to make others happy doesn't make you a good person.

Does that provoke you? A few years ago, those words would have triggered me because I tied my worth to what I could be for others. But I've since learned that was a mistake.

I grew up admiring that trait in my mother. I watched her give herself away until, in the end, she was broken. I still grieve for her pain.

I look at myself, and my brother and sister, and see similar traits in each of us. We all learned to self-sacrifice, to hurt ourselves in the name of love.

But love isn't supposed to hurt. Love is the one thing that doesn't hurt.

Sacrificing yourself does hurt. It leaves you feeling unimportant, walked on, resentful. Ultimately, we are each responsible for teaching those around us how we want to be loved. When we self-sacrifice, we teach others that we have no boundaries and that we can be used.

We teach ourselves lessons, too, about our own worth. When we put ourselves last, we learn that we are unimportant. We don't matter. It took me years to learn that I do matter.

For most of my life, I sought my worth in someone else. I believed if I could only find someone who loved me, I would be worthy. But all along, that person was in the mirror. When I finally realized love was never something I needed to earn—and that I actually deserved to be loved—everything changed.

We accept the love we believe we deserve. And when you grow up believing that love must be earned by how much you can do for others, you end up trapped in an endless cycle of trying to be "good enough".

When I ended that cycle, I stopped trying to earn love. I finally knew what I actually deserved: to be loved as I am. Never was love something I needed to earn.

Love is my birthright, and I deserve it because I am.

I don't think I was ever told I was pretty when I was young.

When I was hitting puberty and starting to grow curves, my dad made comments saying I had a nice body. My dad would say inappropriate things sometimes. We always chalked it up to my awkward father, but looking back I believe those comments stemmed from abuse in his own childhood. I'll never know the truth though. He never said much about his parents except for glowing positivity. Even when he told me the story of his father making him shoot his own wounded dog when he was young, it was never meant to criticize his dad. You never did that.

But my dad's sister had a lot of mental health issues, and some of the stories I heard about her make me believe there was a lot of darkness in my dad's childhood.

When my own daughters were born, I was determined that they would know they were beautiful. I wanted them to have the self-esteem I never had.

In my mid-thirties, during a time when my mental health was struggling with deep depression, a friend set up a photoshoot for me. She did it under the guise of needing photos for her hair and makeup portfolio, but I now believe she saw how broken I was and wanted to help me.

This was close to 20 years ago and it was a pivotal part of my life.

At the time, I didn't own a cell phone and had only heard about something called "Facebook". I set up an account on the family computer and started finding high school friends and family from Nova Scotia. It was a beacon in my lonely life. After years of it just being my kids and I, I could connect with others.

The images from that first shoot were sent to me via Facebook. When I finally saw them something happened to me. It was a realization. I could be pretty.

I had never had much self-esteem when I was younger, and then having two kids and feeling disconnected from my husband didn't help. My roles were mother and wife.

I had disappeared.

And now I was even more flawed. Having children had given me stretch marks and loose skin. My metabolism had changed and I was constantly battling with myself to stay as skinny as possible.

Because, in my mind, skinny equaled beautiful. I remember first starving myself at the age of 7.

But here I was, in my mid-thirties, looking at photos of myself and feeling pretty. Not just pretty but sexy even.

And the best part was they were on Facebook, so all the people I went to school with could see it. Me! Being pretty!

I was hooked at that point. I started finding Facebook groups for tattooed models to join and share my photos.

And then something even crazier happened. Photographers started reaching out to me wanting to take photos of me. Me?!

I chalked it up to my tattoos. At the time I had half sleeves and not many women were as tattooed as I was. I knew that made me unique.

Besides, I could never admit to myself that they wanted photos of me. Insignificant me.

One photoshoot followed another, and I started to make friends. Some of those people are still in my life today.

My husband didn't like my modelling and wanted to control how many photos I posted online. But I was in love. Modelling had entered my life and I wasn't giving it up.

I sent my photos to one of the most prestigious tattoo magazines at the time and they told me they would publish me. I was a *Skin&Ink* doll. After that, I would madly apply to as many magazines as I could. I got accepted. I stopped counting my publications. I credit modelling with building my self-esteem out of nothing.

It wasn't all good, however. There were times when it would actually illuminate my insecurities. I would criticize myself.

Believe I looked fat. Believe that I was only pretty in the photos because the photographer would edit away my ugly flaws.

But it also gave me so many gifts. Friends when I was alone. A way to play and be creative. Confidence.

And the ability to see that I could be pretty.

If you were my friend three or four years ago, you don't know me now.

I think about that sometimes. How much I've changed and what the people who knew me then must think. From the outside in, what does it look like to them?

Not that it matters. Other people's opinions of you are not any of your business.

But three or four years ago I was messy. Drinking daily. Hurting greatly. Still heartbroken. Still lonely. And making mistakes. I certainly wasn't my best.

Two opposite things can be true at the same time, however, because I was also on my way to healing. I was discovering. I was growing. I was learning who I was, and the mistakes I made during that time taught me important lessons. Through them, I learned what I was willing to keep in my life and what I no longer wanted.

Although I was a mess, I was still helping people. I still had wisdom to share. I had already learned so much and I was making a difference.

I was teaching during the week and going home to drink after my classes. I was drinking on the weekends. I was trying to drown my pain in alcohol and I couldn't seem to stop. I'd tell myself I would stop but when I'd finish my classes, the little devil on my shoulder would whisper to me. And I'd walk to the grocery store and get a few beers. Just a couple, I would tell myself.

And then I'd wake the next day feeling guilty and shameful. One truth I've learned is that you can't hate yourself well. It doesn't work that way and if it did, I would be the most healed person in the world.

I had to stop judging myself to get better.

I credit my boyfriend, Dale, with a big part of the healing that I've achieved over the past two years. And going back to my parents' home to face my past.

Dale grounds me. I'm no longer seeking love and that is a huge shift. He gives me stability. Safety.

And facing my family's pain has given me so much understanding. I'm a different person now.

I rarely drink, and when I do, I'm reminded of how I used to feel when I drank all the time. Drinking will give you a dark cloud over your head that doesn't leave, even when you are sober. I think it was a huge part of why I was so lonely.

But I had to go through that to get here. And I love where I am now.

If you knew me then, you don't know me now. The girl you knew then doesn't exist anymore. She is a past incarnation.

I'm grateful for her sacrifice so that I could become who I was meant to be.

Healing is messy.

And I have had so much to heal. For a long time after starting this journey, I was walking wounded. But regardless, I was still teaching other people about self-awareness. My yoga classes are dedicated to this and I truly had so much wisdom to share even though, if you want to know the truth, I was not okay.

I knew I wasn't okay too. But I also knew I was still way better than I had ever been in my life.

You can be both. You can be healing and doing better than you ever have been, and still hurting and in pain, making mistakes.

I look in the mirror now and see a different woman. I can honestly tell you I'm no longer walking wounded. I'm no longer making mistakes. I'm genuinely grounded and solid, and in the best position of my life. I won't tell you I'm healed—there will always be more things to face and I will always be trying to be better, but I feel so proud of where I am now.

Before now, I felt shameful. How could I guide others to love themselves when I was going home every night to drink the pain away? When my heart was still a gaping hole in my chest that I was desperately seeking someone to heal? When I was so overwhelmed with loneliness and pain?

I didn't hide my messiness. I don't think I could have if I tried. I'm not someone who is capable of a facade. I think even when I was still married and trying to hide how bad things were from friends and family, you could still clearly tell we weren't okay. And during my healing, I started to open up and share more and more. Eventually, there wasn't really anything I hid. I actually attribute that vulnerability to how I have been able to learn self-acceptance and self-love. Owning the parts of yourself that you judge and feel shame over is a fierce act of self-love.

I also didn't want to be fake. It was important for me to show myself that this whole journey of vulnerability has been entirely about letting others see themselves in me. If I'm not being genuine, how can that be?

I'm very reflective when it comes to my own journey because it has given me empathy for people around me who I can see the former me within. Walking wounded. Feeling shameful. Trying to run from their pain. Desperately seeking someone to heal their broken hearts.

If my words resonate with you, please know that it gets better. And it got better for me when I stopped running from the pain and stopped looking for anyone else to heal me. I am my own hero. I saved myself. But it was not easy, and I had to experience being messy to learn how to be better.... So let yourself make mistakes. And then get back up and try again.

Don't let self-loathing take you down, please. You deserve the entire world—you just need to remember that.

I reconnected with someone who used to be a close friend of mine recently. Well, kind of. I mean I followed her on Instagram, and she let me. We had a falling out a few years ago. Well, kind of. I mean we were very toxic friends and at some point she blocked me and we stopped communicating.

I'm thankful for that.

This friend is a complicated person to me.

On the one hand, she helped me during a difficult time in my life. I credit her for why I became a model, and I know the things she did for me were out of the kindness of her heart. She saw me struggling and she tried to help me. She was the one to arrange my first ever photoshoot and I will always be grateful to her for that.

Modelling has helped me immensely through my journey. It helped me to look into the mirror and see that I could be beautiful when I believed myself ugly. It gave me confidence and it brought people into my life that I needed. To this day I still have multiple wonderful friends who I know because of modelling.

I've known her for a very long time, 20 years now. We've seen each other go through many phases of life, and she and I have related well to one another.

Like most friendships that have lasted many years, we've gone through periods where we were part of each other's lives and then haven't seen one another for a long time.

I haven't seen her for a long time.

But the last time we were close, we were both very toxic and unwell, and we both made mistakes. This time when we dropped out of each other's lives, I'm pretty sure it was for good.

Even though she "let" me follow her on Instagram, it doesn't mean she wants to be friends again and frankly, I don't blame her. We weren't great together. I am not sure I want to be her friend again.

I only added her because I don't want any more animosity. She has been an important part of my life, and despite what transpired between us, I still care about her and wish her well and happy.

I want to be clear here: what I share next is my perspective. I don't know her side but I'm willing to own my bad behaviour. And I was messy.

We reconnected just as the lockdowns from the pandemic were starting to end and life was coming back to normal. She was recovering from cancer and, at the same time, her marriage was dissolving. She was hurting and trying to find out who she was after years of pain in her life.

Just like me. She was a mirror.

We went out together to the bars. At the time, I was deep in my own pain and drinking a lot. I was lonely and still trying to heal my heart from the person who I had connected to right after my marriage ended. And when we went to the bars, he was a bartender at one of the establishments. So I would see him and so would she.

She's beautiful. Drop dead gorgeous. I was insecure.

But I genuinely loved her and wanted to help her through the process of finding herself again. So I introduced her to a friend of mine who was both a model and a photographer, and the three of us took photos together. Lots of photos. Sexy pictures.

It was fun. And I know that she and I were both seeking attention. Since we were both wounded, those photos were more than just fun for us. We were seeking validation and love.

But I don't think either one of us achieved that. I can tell you what I achieved. Insecurity. Comparison. More self-loathing.

I looked at her body and compared it to mine. She was thinner than I. My whole life, skinny equalled beauty. I had gone through long periods of my life counting every single calorie and working out for hours every day. At the time we began to hang out together, I thought I had healed from that mindset but she triggered it all again.

So photoshoots that started out as "just for fun" started to trigger the fuck out of me.

And we'd go to the bar and she would flirt with the man from my past. The man I still had feelings for and, if I'm being honest, the reason I wanted to go to the bar at all. I wanted him to see me doing well. I wanted to make him jealous.

When I found out that she had him on her Snapchat and was talking to him, I got upset.

After all, I believe in girl code. Friends don't mess around with men that other friends have been with. And she knew my feelings for him. It felt like a huge betrayal.

I gossiped to a mutual friend about her. I wasn't nice. I wasn't a good friend. And shortly afterwards she just dropped from my life. I was blocked.

And I understand. I deserved that. I should have been better.

Looking back, that experience taught me so much. Even though I lost a friend through it, the lessons it taught me are invaluable.

Be impeccable with your word. That's lesson number one and still something I will check myself for at times of frustration. Don't gossip. Speak kindly about people. And if you have a problem with someone, tell them. Don't talk shit about people.

I was upset with her behaviour regarding someone she knew I cared for and I still think I was valid to be so. But I don't know what she chose to actually do with him. I'm pretty certain I triggered her just as much as she triggered me, so maybe her actions were based on her own insecurities. If she could get the man I valued, maybe that would make her feel better. But again, I don't know what happened between them and it doesn't matter anymore.

But the entire situation taught me to be better. It made me revisit my relationship with myself and the comparison game I've played my whole life with other women. It asked me to look at my self-worth and what I believed was attached to it. If I was skinny enough, sexy enough, beautiful enough then I could be chosen and loved.

I'm not mad at her. We were both wounded and doing the best we could during a really hard time. But I don't know if I would want to be friends again, and I'm okay with that too. People come into your life for a reason and I think she came into my life for many reasons.

Now I have a new life far removed from the woman I was back then, and she helped me get there. I wish her happiness and love.

Thanks to the lessons she gave me, I already have mine.

In some people's stories, I'm a villain.

I've learned that you can't control how other people see you. It's been a hard lesson. But one that I can really see around me.

Sometimes, it's a matter of different perspective. You might see my actions as incorrect. I might believe I acted fairly.

Sometimes I legitimately make mistakes. I am human and healing and I've done things I now realize weren't right. Those are lessons to learn from and to try to make amends for.

Sometimes it's an entirely different story. A story that feels to you like fantasy. Those moments are confusing and yet when someone has made up their mind about you, you can't do anything about it.

The truth is that each of us has an entirely different experience in this world. I see the world through my eyes, painted by my previous life experiences and beliefs and my own mental health, plus anything else that could cause me to see you in a different light. Good or bad.

Maybe you had a bad experience with a short, tattooed girl and now you expect all of them to do you wrong.

And the deeper truth is that each of us sees ourselves as the protagonist of the story. We play the role of hero and sometimes victim but each of us sees the world through our own reflection.

We often decide consciously or unconsciously to change details to suit our narrative because, again, this is our story painted by our light.

I've personally experienced a few of these scenarios.

One situation happened when I had a falling out with someone I trusted. She took private conversations and embellished them to fit her narrative and told them to others. I lost a good friend who decided to believe her.

But I must own my part, which means understanding that if I had been impeccable with my words, I would have never shared anything personal with her and she wouldn't have had anything to embellish. It was a hard lesson.

But other scenarios have happened where the story someone has of me doesn't at all match my memory. As far as I'm concerned, it never happened. And yet, I can't change someone else's mind. They believe what they believe.

So, I must make peace with being a villain in their story….

Knowing that I'm still a complicated, but well-intentioned hero in mine.

"You had the power all along."

Words hold such power for me, and that sentence rocked my world. It was said to me by an older woman who swept her way into my life at the most important time. I believe to this day she was God-sent. An earth angel. And she helped me in ways that I desperately needed.

At the time, I was teaching yoga at a gym and she was a regular gym attendant. Since we saw one another so often we had become friends, and we would have many random conversations.

But one fateful day she became more than a friend.

My marriage and home life were crumbling. I mean, we hadn't been good for years but an accumulation of devastating events had really caused us to fall apart.

We were both struggling. Hard. And I was going to work and trying to be ok.

Thank God for my job. At the time I was still new to teaching yoga but it was helping me. The years of my toxic marriage had taken a toll on my soul, and when I first started teaching I was barely breathing. I had no self-confidence and no voice. Teaching was giving those things back to me.

But I was overcome with anger towards my husband. The anger was like a poison in my system.

One fateful day, she saw me.

I was at the gym, running to the bathroom after teaching a class and being bombarded by text messages from my husband. I was trying to reach the privacy of a bathroom stall before I let my tears fall. And she saw.

She took time for me. After all, this wasn't her first encounter with people in pain. She was a retired social worker. She had seen it all. And she, herself, had been through her own hell on earth. She came from a history of alcoholism and domestic abuse. She saw herself in me.

We would meet at a coffee shop, and I would spew my anger to her and tell her how wronged I had been. I was so good at playing the victim. She listened but she never sugar-coated anything, and she called me out when I needed it. That was a gift, and to this day I am grateful for that.

She gave me courage. She gave me honesty. And she showed me I was not alone. But most importantly she taught me that this was my life and if I wanted differently, I needed to choose it. I believe that God will send you the people you need, and most of all, I believe she was sent to me to show me:

"You had the power all along".

Logically, I know it was never ever ever my responsibility to make my mother happy. I still carry guilt. I moved away. I left her. Yes, to build a life that I was deserving of building. Yes, to have my own family. Regardless, I know that she was alone. I know that all she ever wanted was family. And we all left her, my sister to Vancouver Island with her two kids, and my brother to the Okanagan to chase inspirations of building a business. I moved the longest distance away. To Ontario, Canada.

History repeats unless someone becomes aware.

I realize that I also had my children in hope that it would mean I would not be alone. The decision to get pregnant was because I was sad. At the time, my husband and I were attempting to try to build a successful business. He had opened up a small video game store, but we didn't know what we were doing and we gave up everything to do it. We were forced to move in with his parents.

It was during this time that I saw a different side of him. When my husband was under stress, he became hyper-critical and mean. I was very sensitive and this destroyed me. I no longer had any place that felt like home, and the man I loved made me feel horrible. And to top it off, I had a retail job at a clothing store and my boss chose to hate me. I couldn't do anything right. I remember hiding in the bathroom because I also couldn't show anyone I wasn't okay and crying. I would have to wipe my face, and to the very best of my ability, go back out in the world and pretend I was alright.

But I wasn't.

Then one fateful day, I somehow got it in my head that if I had a baby, it would love me. That baby would never leave me. I would never be alone.

Looking at my own mom's life, I think she did the same thing as I did. She had my siblings and me in an attempt to never be alone. She also moved far away from her own mother, and I know my dad and her were never good. My mom was sad. And we all left her.

My kids left me too.

It's wrong to have children with the belief that your children will bring you happiness. Your happiness should never be your child's responsibility. I see this now. I look at my daughters and see them both impacted by the decision I made, and I am doing my best to change the pattern.

They are not responsible for my wellness. They are allowed to live their lives even if that means I don't see them as often. What I want for my daughters now is their happiness. And I'm taking care of mine.

I have not seen my oldest daughter for almost a year. I've reach out and get pushed away. She is very angry with me and I have to understand that I am not in control of her perspective of me. But from my honest perspective, I absolutely know I made mistakes. I was a hover mom to her. I was controlling. I had some nasty toxic traits that I've had to take responsibility for.

But everything I ever did was with misguided love. I love my daughters with everything I am.

I'm still releasing my guilt over my actions. I know I did the best I knew how back then, but I was so very broken and hurting. We can only give what we have, and what I had to give was my own self-loathing and brokenness. I had been raised with guilt, and guilt is what I gave my kids.

I see it still living in them today.

But here's the thing, now that my children are grown, THEIR happiness is also not my responsibility. This is something I am trying to accept. My girls have their own journeys to take, and while it's so hard for me to watch them hurt, I know the lessons are in the pain. I would not have learned myself without all the pain I've been through.

Pain is a great teacher.

The greatest act of love I can do for my girls now is to set them free. To trust in their inherent wisdom and to trust they will be okay. I'm breaking the chains of the past for them because my girls deserve the world.

"You have come so far in your life and past so many obstacles. You have fought for yourself and built a life you're proud of. Of course I'm proud of you"

I woke up to the message above from a dear friend who has known me for a long time. When we met I was still married, not even teaching yoga yet. She has seen me go from where I was to where I am now. She even lived with me shortly after I left my marriage.

She has seen me stuck in an unhappy marriage. She has seen me hating myself. She has seen me messy and sad and drinking too much.

To be told that she is proud of me really hit me….

I mean, I'm also proud of myself. I'm the only one who knows what it's taken to get here. How many tears I've shed. How much I've had to face. It's been one hell of a journey.

A journey that I am so grateful for.

When I was in my marriage, I thought my husband was to blame for my unhappiness, and if I left him everything would be better—sunshine and roses. Little did I know that my journey was only starting. Leaving him meant facing me, and when I had to face me, I had to take ownership of the part I played.

One of the single most humbling things is to face yourself.

Face your own toxic traits. Face the things you did that hurt people you love. Face the things you've been running from for years.

All while trying to figure out how to love yourself when my whole life I hadn't. My whole life!

Facing where you have made mistakes AND forgiving yourself. Having compassion for yourself is one of the hardest things I learned how to do.

Because my guilt is still present.... It's so difficult to confront the fact that your actions hurt someone that you love so much. But I HAD to. It has been an important part of my healing and it's given me the grace to forgive those who have harmed me.

Most people don't intentionally hurt other people. But when you yourself are coming from a past where you have been hurt by people who were supposed to love you, it's all you know. And we only can do what we know.

My parents loved me AND hurt me. My ex loved me AND hurt me. I loved my kids AND hurt them.

It is a truth I've had to face in order to learn to do better, and I want to do better! I will walk through the pain so that I can do better! Not only for me but for my daughters who should have seen their mother love herself instead of hate herself.

I can't change the past no matter how much I want to. I can only change today. And I'm making myself a better person every single day.

For my kids.

I have abandoned myself most of my life. I gave myself away. I did things I didn't want to do to make others happy. I've put my own needs aside. I haven't been great at taking care of myself.

I was too busy taking care of everyone else.

It is crazy how these beliefs form. The belief that sacrificing myself for those I love made me a good person. What it actually made me was resentful. Sad. It made me feel unimportant. And I was angry that no one else seemed to see me and my needs.

I took care of everyone else but who took care of me? I've learned there is a term for my behaviour: toxic empathy. Giving of yourself to your own detriment and then being upset when others don't do the same for you.

When we expect anything from others, we set ourselves up for disappointment. When you give, it should always be from a place of no expectation. Just love. And if you are giving from an empty cup, then you are hurting yourself and that isn't something to feel proud of.

Lessons learned.

But I think my biggest motivation for giving myself away was to be loved. I thought if I did enough for someone, they would see my worth and I'd be loved. And I also believed that I needed to do that. My worth was attached to what I could do or be for someone else. Love wasn't something I deserved without being "good" enough to receive.

I remember crying to another creator's TikTok video. She said I didn't have to earn my worth, and that deserving love was a birthright. The thought was profound and brought me to tears.

Old habits die hard and it is still easy for me to fall into old patterns. After all, my whole life I watched my mom do the same. It's what I grew up believing women were supposed to do, give themselves away.

But one constant truth I see now is that when you bring light to an area of your life that you want to heal, awareness alone can kick-start the process.

Every day I'm healing and learning to stop abandoning me.

I've had some really big lessons since leaving my marriage. And there is one in particular that's been on my mind.

Surviving losing people.

I've lost a lot since making the choice to lose my ex-husband. The first loss I chose, the rest I certainly did not.

Leaving my ex changed everything, including the relationship I had with my daughters. Prior to that, my kids and I were very close. When I left their dad, everything changed. I understand that this happened for two reasons. I chose to leave their dad. And my daughters are now adult women with their own lives.

I have grieved for what was. It's taken me a long time to reconcile that change.

In the four years since a lot more has happened. I've lost friendships. Important friendships. Including my childhood best friend who I never ever thought I would lose.

I've tried to date and meet the right person and have had repeated failed relationships. Those losses have hurt as well, most of all because I had a deep-seated fear of being alone, and they would also reinforce my belief that no one wanted me.

And my mom passed away. My mom was always there for me. She had always been so much more than my mom—she was my best friend. I heard it recently said that no partner will ever love you more than your mom, and knowing how I feel about my kids, and how my mom loved me, I do believe this.

I'm not telling you about my loss wanting you to feel sorry for me. I am sharing this because this was a huge lesson for me. I used to believe I would die if I lost the people I love. It was my greatest fear, and I actually believe I manifested it.

But I lost everything and I'm still standing.

I didn't die.

I'm still here. I'm still full of love. I've lost people and gained others. I now understand that this is a part of life, and that we don't get anyone forever.

I feel differently about my relationships today. I now have a man who I know loves me and has no intention of leaving me. But I've learned that if he left, I would be okay. I know this because losing everything taught me so.

Losing everything forced me to learn how to be there for myself. I've learned that eventually, everyone will abandon you. But if you learn to not abandon yourself you will be okay.

I've stopped abandoning myself.

And I found out I'm still okay.

I have a fear of abandonment. Have. Present tense.

And while I've worked on this fear, the years after ending my marriage made this fear worse, not better.

I think having a fear of abandonment is a very human thing, and many of us have it. Many of us started carrying it as children when our parents were unable to meet our needs. We were left to figure out how to be okay, and since we all crave to be loved, we learned to do what we needed to in order to receive it.

Funny thing is, this looks like abandoning yourself.

I'm pretty certain that is how my fear started. But over the years, it has shown up in my life as people-pleasing. I would do anything to receive your approval. Just love me. Please.

When I made the decision to leave my marriage, I lost more than just a husband. The relationship with my children blew up and there was a period of time where I lost both of them.

They are my life and losing them hurt.

Over the last five years, I've made friendships and had them dissolve. I've put myself out there and dated and felt not chosen. But one of the hardest things I had to face was the holidays.

Christmas. Thanksgiving. Birthdays.

Spending holidays alone when you already feel alone just amplifies everything.

Last Christmas was my first Christmas with my boyfriend, Dale, and it was wonderful. I wasn't alone. And selfishly I had him all to myself as his mom wasn't here and his family doesn't necessarily celebrate Christmas because they are Hindu.

This year, I must share him with his family. When he told me, I could instantly feel myself getting triggered. His parents are visiting for the holidays and the family will be celebrating together.

I understand that in order to heal my fears, I must face them. I also know that I'm triggered. The feelings that I am experiencing are not about Dale. He isn't doing anything wrong and I know he won't just abandon me for the holidays completely. And even if he did, I still have my youngest daughter who I know will celebrate with me.

I am not alone.

And even if I was, I'd be okay.

But I guess it is a reminder of what is gone. How life has changed and will never be the same.

I'm still learning how to be okay with that. I'm also still learning how to be alone.

What matters most in the end?

I've thought about this a lot over the last few years. I've been here 52 years. I've made a few mistakes. No, I've made a lot of mistakes. I've not always done the right thing, but at the time I thought it was. Or, at the time, I was blinded by my pain.

I've made amends with myself for the past—mostly. I think guilt is something that has been ingrained in me by my ancestors, so it's a hard one to release.

Yet, if I were to suddenly die today, I would know that I tried my hardest to be a good person. My mistakes taught me what really matters to me and I've changed because of them.

When I was a little girl, all I wanted was love. I've been chasing love my entire life and I now have it. In multiple ways. I have friends who are like my family. I'm gratefully building a healing relationship with my daughter. And of course, there is Dale. From childhood I dreamt of a man who would sweep me off my feet.

I always thought I would know immediately when I met the "one." And Dale and I did have our moment when we met at the water fountain and our eyes locked—we both knew (I'll tell that story fully in the next chapter).

And while I still believe we both knew in that moment; the love I have for him now took time to grow. It wasn't love at first sight. He and I built what we have now.

Every day it feels stronger. I have never felt so close to another person.

But if I were to die today, I think I'd be okay with the legacy I'd leave behind. For the last 5 years I've worked so hard to be a better person. To learn from my mistakes and to make amends. To help others.

I would hope I'd be remembered for being kind. I hope I would leave some people better for knowing me.

There are some things I can't take back and I hope that I'd be forgiven.

But I live every day with the best intentions and pride in who I've become. That's all I can do.

And for me, that is enough.

It’s been a year since that last visit to see my dad in the hospital. It's been over two years since my mom passed away. It's been five years since I left my marriage.

When I look back over those years, I see so much change. The girl I see in the mirror has grown up. No longer am I a woman-child living in fear and self-loathing.

I know my worth is not attached to what I can be for someone else.

I know that I’m beautiful even with my flaws.

I’ve learned that I am capable of doing hard things.

I’ve learned that I am okay alone.

And most of all, I forgive myself for the past—understanding I’ve always done the best I could. But I’m doing better now.

I also know that I’m still growing and changing and healing. And I’m at peace with that. I’ve come a long way from the girl I used to be.

And I’m proud of the woman I now see in the mirror.

She deserves the world, she always has. She just didn’t know.

But now that she does, it’s my job to give it to her.

Reborn

If you knew me yesterday you don't know me now

The tides have come in and swept the old me away

I was washed with fire and wind

I was destroyed so I could become something new

If you knew me yesterday you met the girl who was my sacrifice

She died so that I could be born.

Finding Love

Dancing for Love

Dancing for love
Swirling in hopes someone would see my beauty
Would notice me
Would see me
Love me, please
Love me, please
I spun circles hoping…

No one saw

My dance was futile

Endless

Impossible

I stopped the dance
I stopped spinning
I stopped swirling

And you saw
Not my beauty
But my soul

And that was better.

Five years ago I made the scariest decision of my life by ending my marriage. I was afraid that by choosing to leave, I would be alone forever. After all, who would want me? I was 46, and when I looked in the mirror, I didn't see a person of value. I definitely didn't see my worth, so who else would? I don't think anyone wants to be alone for the rest of their lives, but I feared that that would be my fate.

I had hit rock bottom. Rock bottom is the most painful place in the world, yet also one of the most powerful. At rock bottom, you really only have two choices: stay and die because the pain is too great, or change.

I chose to change.

But my whole life, I only wanted love. Even when I was a young girl, I fantasized about finding someone who would love me unconditionally, just the way I was. I hadn't felt loved in my marriage. I felt alone. Unwanted. Invisible.

After making the decision to leave my marriage, I entered a whole new world. A world of dating. The world had drastically changed since I was last single and I was entering it broken. A bare shell of a human. 27 years in a broken marriage had taken its toll on me.

I made poor decisions. I continued to let people hurt me. Repeatedly. Until I learned better.

"Finding Love" is my story of coming to realize why I had so much trouble finding love and then, finally succeeding in finding it.

It tells the story of me finding my current boyfriend, Dale, who happens to be twenty years younger than I am, and it shares my thoughts as I process what it means to be in love again after a lifetime of failed love.

And my attempts to do it right this time.

I believe that over the last few years and in my late 40s, I have had to learn how to be loved, and even now, at 52, I'm still learning.

I never felt truly loved in my marriage. After leaving my ex, and when I began to date seeking love, I had repeated failures. I felt unwanted. I felt used.

They say that whatever you saw as love before the age of seven becomes your subconscious beliefs about what love is supposed to be.

I saw my mom sacrifice herself for us. I saw my dad put his needs and wants first and the rest of us last. He was the man of the house and that meant certain privileges. He saw the world in a very traditional way, and despite the fact that I despised my parents' dynamic, my subconscious brain still believed that was what love was.

I recreated it in my marriage. And once single, I chose men who also put their needs first and disregarded mine.

It wasn't until two years ago, the summer my mom passed away that I made a massive self-discovery. I realized that watching my dad put himself above my mom had created a subconscious belief within me that this is what men do.

When I came home, I came home differently, and I was no longer willing to let men hurt me.

That awareness changed my life. Since then, I have dated only two people.

The first relationship ended pretty quickly after realizing that I once again was choosing someone who couldn't put me first.

After I chose to end that relationship, the second one showed up in my life a few months later.

His name is Dale.

One fateful day, he was standing at the water fountain at my place of work while I was running past to the bathroom. Our eyes met and I had this overwhelming knowing. He must have felt it too because later that night, once I was home, he messaged me online. He was an acquaintance who I hadn't really thought of before, but on that night, there was something different.

I believe it's because I was finally ready.

I've heard it said that we all have three major loves in our lives. I'm not sure I believe that, as we are all on such different journeys, but in my life, this is actually true.

They say that your first love is your introduction to love. It can happen in high school, and it's your idea of what love should be. It is love idealized, and it is based on fantasy, not reality.

I met my ex-husband in high school and fell for him madly. At the time, I believed that we were going to have this perfect life with two and a half kids and a picket fence. We kind of had that, until it all fell apart. We were just children ourselves, without any understanding of how to communicate or even love one another. It was a painful 27 years that we stayed together. I think that both of us clung to that ideal. Both of our parents stayed together until death do us part.

It was what we were supposed to do.

When I left him, I broke the tradition.

Your second love comes with painful lessons. They sweep you off your feet and then break you down. It can be passionate but painful, and can be filled with abuse and manipulation. It starts with you falling for them but ends with you learning how to love yourself.

This describes the man who came into my life after I ended my marriage. He swept me off my feet months after leaving my ex-husband. At the time, I was definitely not looking to fall in love and he came out of nowhere. After 27 years of being married but feeling so alone, meeting him woke desires in me that had been stagnant for so long. It was a toxic, intense connection that took me two years to overcome, but when I did, I walked away choosing me.

Your third love is the love of your life. They aren't at all what you expect, and they also come out of nowhere, but somehow it just fits. It's easy. You don't have to fight for this love. They are your safe place, and the love you experience with them is unconditional.

This describes Dale and I perfectly. I actually knew who Dale was before we got together. He had seen me at the mall one day and I guess I left an impression. He sought me out, found me on social media, and asked if I would have coffee with him. But during this time, I was just beginning the toxic run I had with love number two. And while I thought he was cute, I was suspicious of his intentions, and I considered him too young for me. So I denied him.

But four years later, on a fateful June day, he was at the water fountain at my work, our eyes met and I knew.

Nothing is perfect and we've had our moments, but we communicate about everything and I trust him—I love the man he is. I also feel so loved by him, which is new for me. In both previous relationships, I didn't feel wanted or loved. But I know Dale loves me. He has even told me he sees me as his future wife.

I know he and I have a good life ahead and I believe he is my love number three- the one that is meant to be.

He is the love of my life.

The months after ending my marriage I was in full survival mode. I couldn't eat. I couldn't sleep. I literally felt like I was vibrating. I couldn't afford to move out of our house so we were stuck living together. He moved his stuff downstairs and I stayed in my daughter's bedroom.

I was teaching as many classes as possible and trying not to be home.

I was losing weight.

I had blinders on, just trying to keep breathing.

And someone saw me. He was a member at the gym I taught for. He started to pursue me. He was tall, handsome and younger than I was. And he kept coming. He approached me several times trying to talk to me, he even started to take my classes.

I was still oblivious, not thinking anyone would be interested in me. I was just trying to continue to put one foot in front of the other. I had no time to look for love, and it was the last thing on my mind.

But one fateful day, it found me.

He took two of my classes back-to-back. The first was a spin class, and only he showed up. He made me nervous and shy, but I taught the class and finished with a bit of time before my next class, which was yoga. He stayed with me. We talked and he flirted. He told me that happy baby was his favourite yoga pose and I laughed. He obviously didn't realize which pose that was.

It was sinking in that he liked me.

He came to my yoga class too. I was teaching about solar plexus that night and the room was full. So when I cued happy baby, I could hear him snicker as he realized that happy baby is the pose where you lie on your back and expose your bum by drawing your knees into your armpits, holding your feet like a "happy baby."

When the class ended, I shared one of my favourite quotes from Maya Angelou:

"God put rainbows in the clouds so that in the darkest and dreariest of moments, we could see a possibility of hope."

And I suggested that we should aspire to be "rainbows" in other people's clouds. That we should look to help others and give them hope.

The class ended and he left without saying anything. I was kind of disappointed. But when everyone left, he came back and said one thing to me.

"Thank you for being a rainbow in my cloud."

Something happened at that moment. I couldn't stop thinking about him, and that night I sought him out online. We started talking and would continue to do so until the sun rose.

I had never done that before.

I don't believe in accidents, and this man was meant to come into my life. Shortly after this beautiful meeting, everything would fall apart. But not before he awoke in me something I thought I lost.

Love. Desire. Butterflies.

But you attract what you are, and I was walking wounded back then. Broken. A bare shell of a human. So was he.

I couldn't believe this beautiful man wanted me, and since I hadn't felt like this in decades, I was afraid I'd never feel it again. I clung to him even though he hurt me. Repeatedly.

We did an off-and-on toxic dance for two years before I finally said no to him. Saying no to him was saying yes to me, and that changed everything. But it was hard because I loved him.

I had to love me more.

Some people come into your life to teach you, and sometimes the lessons are painful. It took time, but I can honestly say I am grateful for it all now.

Especially since it led me to the man I have now, and to finally knowing what it feels like to actually be loved.

I've mentioned that Dale and I met at the water fountain at my place of work. I also shared that we met officially right after I ended my marriage.

Fast forward four years and a lot of work towards healing trauma, and that night at the water fountain was the right time.

Four years of on-and-off dating, loneliness and heartbreak had taught me a lot of lessons. The biggest of all was how to love myself. That one changed everything.

They say we attract our own mirrors. Our vibration attracts others with the same vibration. I believe it.

I see it in Dale.

When we met, we were both kind of sad. We both were having difficulties with previous close friendships and were missing people that we used to be close with.

Dale's identical twin was facing some serious health concerns, and my dad was in the hospital with dementia.

In the beginning, I gave Dale a bit of a hard time. I had been hurt enough times that, if he wasn't able to make me a priority, I didn't need him. I would rather be alone than be with someone who wasn't going to choose me.

But he kept trying. He kept proving to me he wanted me.

After a while, I dropped my walls.

Even so, we went through our challenges. I went home to see my dad in the hospital. My youngest daughter moved in with us after she broke up with her fiancé. My dog got really sick and needed expensive surgery.

And he was there. I wasn't alone.

And that felt new.

I had some heavy conversations with Dale recently.

I believe that we all wish someone could see us—the real us, in all our ugliness—and still love us.

So I told him some things from my past. Some of them are things I'm not proud of. I told him these things because I wanted him to know me. Not just the person I am now, but the person I was. And how I have become the person I am now.

I wanted him to understand.

It was daunting. I've made mistakes. I haven't always been good. And I think we are all afraid that who we truly are can't be loved.

But I've done enough healing to understand that the right person will love you regardless. Maybe this was my test to see if he truly could love all of who I am.

So I told him and he responded with no judgement. He had sympathy for what I've been through and, in turn, he opened up to me.

It was healing for me, and I believe we are even closer than before.

If my mom was still here, I think she'd like him.

They say you aren't capable of loving someone until you learn to love yourself.

I never understood this.

I mean, I have hated myself my whole life, and yet I felt I fiercely loved others. Sometimes to my own detriment.

It took me time, but I think I understand now. Let me rephrase that sentence.

You aren't capable of loving someone UNCONDITIONALLY until you learn to love yourself.

Because before I learned how to love myself, my love came with conditions.

Love me back.

Before I learned how to love myself I was looking for someone to fill the holes in my heart. Someone to make me whole. Someone to make me feel like I mattered. Because I didn't believe I did.

And because I wasn't giving myself the love I really needed—my own—I was so love-starved, looking for my heart to be healed.

But real love comes from a space of not needing anything back. From wholeness. Real love sets you free. It doesn't cling. It doesn't hold. And it doesn't have expectations.

That kind of love is rare.

I'm not even sure I have it yet because I still want to be loved back.

But I'm close.

I believe our souls chose to be here to experience love. I believe love is the single most important thing we have. But opening your heart is always a risk.

It's humans at their most vulnerable.

And all of us get to experience pain here. Rejection. Abandonment. Betrayal. Yes, I'm referring to romantic love, but we can also experience that pain in family and friends, and your childhood is the stepping stone for your adult relationships.

I felt rejected as a little girl. Never good enough. Never wanted. The kid who was awkward and clumsy and chubby who crushed hard on a boy in class who definitely didn't like me back. The kid picked last for any team. The ugly nerd. So that is also how I felt as an adult. I see the clear correlation now. And it was not until I could see that, that I began to change this in my life.

Even when I was married to a man who I now understand did love me the best he was able to, I never felt enough. Loved. Desired. Wanted.

But I now see this was my self-fulfilling prophecy. This is what I believed about myself so this is what I created in my life.

When I changed that belief, I changed my life.

Self-love changes everything. When you finally believe you deserve to be loved, then love will find you.

I see it to be true in my own life. When I learned how to love myself, it found me.

As I write these words, Dale sleeps beside me. I think he sometimes wakes up wondering what I'm going to write today. I write every single morning, and this ritual is a huge part of my continued healing. It is me looking into the mirror and processing what looks back.

We have a 20-year age gap which means nothing to us right now but does matter to some family. And in the future, this could impact us. I know this.

But I love this man more than anything. I see my future with him.

In my past, I can see how I never actually loved the men in my life. I loved the facade of them. What I wanted them to be. And when that failed me I was left broken and sad and believing I was still unwanted.

But I love Dale. I see myself in him in so many ways. Yes, we have differences but we are also the same person. We feel things deeply. We love hard. Sometimes to our own detriment.

He's goofy. Ridiculous. Clumsy. Amazing. Sometimes I watch that man's antics and love pours from me. I love him so much. And in a really weird way, because I can see myself in him, loving him is also like loving myself.

This relationship is different because I am different now. I'm healed enough to believe something new for myself—I am worthy, beautiful and wanted. Dale mirrors that back to me, showing me every day that my new beliefs are true.

It only took me 52 years to figure it out, but all things happen in divine timing. And I share my story with you in hopes that if you can see yourself in me, you can see this in your own life sooner than I did.

Remember, you are worthy, wanted and beautiful, and YOU DESERVE THE WORLD.

One of my coworkers just got engaged. She came to work with a giant rock on her finger. I've watched her romance from a distance, with my own opinions, and without going into details, I'm not sure it meets my personal values.

I try not to judge, but I find my own beliefs definitely coming up.

She is close to my age with adult kids, like me, and this is, from a distance, a whirlwind romance. They've only been together for two months.

My parents also only dated for two months before they said their vows, and they were together until my mom passed 60 years later.

Should they have stayed together? That's another question.

I didn't hold my tongue when I saw the ring like perhaps I should have.

Sometimes I have that problem.

So when she said, "When you know you know," especially at her age, I countered with "At my age, I'm way more careful."

I was 19 when I got married, and definitely not wise enough to make that decision.

I used to romanticize my parents. I used the same term: when you know, you know. And I also believed that I would know instantly when I met my forever person.

And yes, I knew something when I saw Dale at the water fountain at my work. There was a moment.

But love? Love takes time. And when you go through things together, it grows. Especially when you have experienced going through things alone. You must trust them, but when you have been hurt, sometimes that takes time.

Having Dale beside me this past year and a half and facing difficult times together has bonded me to him. And that didn't happen overnight.

I think it had to take time because of the pain of my past. I made Dale show me that he was here to stay.

I had been abandoned enough in my past. I needed to see that he would stay. And he has.

Every day my love grows for him. He's my home. And I think my love will just keep growing.

Now I believe good things take time.

When I was really lonely, I would see posts on social media that said

"One day you will wake up at 11:30 on a Sunday with the love of your life and you'll get up and make pancakes… and it'll be alright"

I would always repost it in hopes that someday it would come true.

Over the last few years, I have written many things in my journal, including my dreams. One thing I would write over and over is a wish. I wanted to dance in the kitchen with the love of my life while we made dinner….

I think that post on social media I used to wish for came true for me.

Only it was a Monday night instead of a Sunday morning, and instead of pancakes, it was some hamburger helper.

There are 20 years between Dale and I.

I have mentioned this before, but I don't think I have ever written about what that actually means. For us, at this stage in our relationship, we don't think about it much. We've been together for a year and a half now and are about to share our second Christmas together.

But to other people, this may seem crazy.

And at first, it was a concern of mine. After all, a woman in her 50s has different life goals than a man in his 30s. What if he wants children? My kids are grown. My oldest daughter is 3 years younger than him. That ship has sailed for me, and I care too much for Dale to make him miss out on his own opportunity to be a father. It took time, but he eventually convinced me that he is okay with never being a dad. My dog and cats have become his babies. Truly. Watching him with my pets makes me love him more.

But there are other concerns that almost prevented us from staying together in the beginning.

He is very close to his family, in particular his mom, and she wasn't very approving. I can understand. She's only 8 years older than I am. I know it's not a typical relationship and probably not what she expected for her son.

But his mom is a wonderful woman, and despite not exactly loving our relationship, she has respected his decision to choose me.

She is very kind to me.

There are other members of his family who don't approve either, but they have less impact on his life. Because of this, though, he was reluctant to go public with our relationship.

That bothered me and was something we have had to work through. I think we have come to a place of resolution now.

I'm sure people talk. I'm sure they gossip. Let them. I don't care.

I don't live my life for the approval of others.

But I don't think I can responsibly make the decision to be in a relationship with such a large age gap without at least giving thought to what that means.

I am aware of getting older. I see the lines around my eyes and on my forehead. I would be lying if I said it doesn't bother me.

After all, in my first marriage, my ex made comments about believing that he would lose attraction for me if I gained too much weight or got too many tattoos. My appearance mattered, and I would lose his love if I changed.

This is a huge trigger for me.

And then, there is the future. Right now, I'm 52 and he is 32. We are both vibrant and healthy. But in 20 years, I'll be 72 and he will be my age. What will that mean for us?

But I have a belief that surpasses all of my worries.

Life is meant to be LIVED. I wasted enough years unhappy. I have spent the majority of my life giving myself away for others and not pursuing my own happiness.

It's my turn now.

And yes, things could go wrong. Who knows what the future holds for us. But if I didn't take a chance and had chosen not to be with Dale, I would have missed out on us.

He's the first person I've ever felt loved by and safe with, and that's all I ever wanted.

Why would I miss out on that?

I woke up to Dale dropping kisses all over me. Sometimes I am amazed by where I am now. This handsome silly dorky man at my side. And how much I love him. It's overwhelming sometimes.

It's been a year and a half now since he and I started dating. In the beginning, we were all over each other. I think that's pretty normal. Any new couple goes through that phase where they can't get enough of one another—the minute they are alone, they are ripping each other's clothes off.

But life happens. My youngest daughter moved in with us and we had a lot of adjustments and stress, and the honeymoon phase seemed to end.

Lately, though, we have been getting our second wind. And it's been wonderful. It's different than the first time because we now know one another, and that does change the sex. But it's like we have this hunger that can't be satisfied. I like it. A lot!

The relationship I have with Dale isn't like anything I have ever experienced. Yes, I mentioned sex, but in all honesty that's such a small aspect of our relationship. The bigger aspects are our openness and connection. I've never been with anyone I've felt this comfortable with. We talk about everything. I can be myself entirely around him.

He is a huge part of my life. I wake up beside him and go to sleep beside him. Every day we talk throughout. I can't even fathom life without him now.

And yes, we have some difficulties, some of which I'm not sure how to resolve, but I think I've found my future in him. I think he and I will be together. I don't see an end in sight.

And I don't know what that will look like but I'm grateful for it all.

At the age of 52, Dale is the first person I genuinely feel loved by.

I'm not saying he is the first person to love me. I'm saying he's the first one to make me feel loved.

Looking back, I know my ex loved me the best way he could. But I was broken and so was he and so was our love.

I don't think he could have loved me in a way that I would have been able to receive. My own beliefs that told me I was unlovable got in the way.

What you think, you create.

I created a story where I didn't matter and no one wanted me, and that became my reality. Whether it was true or not was a different story, but it created a wall around me that love couldn't enter.

Change your beliefs and change your life.

When I healed from all that self-loathing and learned that I actually do matter, I was able to let Dale in. And he shows me every day that I am loved.

But I do believe that it all began with my own self-love journey so that I could let others love me too.

Today is the fifth anniversary of my move from my ex's house to my apartment. Five years here.

I still love this place. It's my first home entirely on my own. Before this, I only knew living with my ex and my parents.

It was the first place I ever got to decorate and I manifested what I wanted. In the months before moving in, I repeatedly wrote in my journal: tapestries and crystals. I have those.

These walls have seen a lot.

The first year was the discovery of how much I needed to heal. I had conflicts with my oldest daughter who moved in with me and then left with her boyfriend months later. It was dramatic and painful and I was a mess.

The years that followed saw the pandemic and the lockdowns. I was alone a lot and I was lonely. But, in time, I learned how to make peace with that.

I had my first big birthday party here, celebrating my 49th birthday. It was a new life.

I had been embarrassed of my old home and I would have never invited anyone over. It was a mess no matter how much I tried to clean. Plus my ex was extremely introverted and would not have been pleased with company.

There were a lot of things I hid back then.

But now I was free and I could do whatever I wanted! I had never experienced that before and I loved it. I took back my life in this home. I found out who I was, and it wasn't the girl who was trying her whole life to be good enough to be loved.

There were many tears. I grieved for my mom in this apartment. I drank wine in the bathtub and I screamed at God.

But I also learned how to forgive myself here. To have compassion for myself here. And I learned how to love myself.

After I learned how to love myself, I learned how to love Dale. It's now been over a year since he made his first visit to my little apartment, and that visit was the first of many. Over the last 8 months, he has moved in.

Now my tapestries and crystals have been joined with his belongings.

In a week, he and I will take our first vacation together. We are flying to Florida to see his mom and go to Universal.

Over the years, there were two other things I would write in my journal, and today, I can happily say I have them both:

A hot man and travel.

Here's to a beautiful life.... Continued.

HERO

Don't be my hero
I saved me long ago
Just be by my side
And love me as I am
Don't come and rescue me
I can do that on my own
Let's go on adventures
Together lets explore the world
Don't try to make me happy
I can do that all alone
Just laugh and cry with me
Sharing the good and bad
Come live your life with me
I don't need you
I just want you
I don't need a hero
I just want you by my side

Finding Life

Alone Together

I found myself

In a crowd of people walking alone, together
Silently suffering with smiles painted on
Hiding ourselves, convinced no one would understand
Each of us lost in our own pain
Thinking no one would understand
All of us, suffering the same…

Walking alone, together.

I used to think that I would never do anything big. My role in the world was to be a mother. I created two beautiful women, and they would be the ones to make a difference. My role was to nurture them.

And that was enough. Still is. My daughters are still the most important things I've ever created.

But I had no idea where my life would lead after I had the courage to jump into the unknown.

Leaving my marriage was the bravest thing I've ever done, and because I was brave, I believe I was rewarded.

In the past five years since I've built a yoga career I'm proud of, become a reiki master and a meditation guide, co-hosted a retreat, co-hosted programs designed to help women face trauma, been interviewed for podcasts, built a large TikTok following, I am about to be a two-time published author. I've spoken in front of large groups of people and most of all, I've connected with people.

I've helped people who are in pain like I once was.

Me!

Little insignificant me.

I've also lived like I never have before. I've gone dancing, sang at a karaoke bar and gotten over the voice in my head that told me people were judging me. While those things may seem small to you, this has been huge in my journey.

All of this beautiful life was waiting for me on the other side of fear.

There is a quote that struck such a chord in my soul because of its truth.

"Courage is not something you get before you do something scary. It's what you get after."

"Finding Life" captures my reflections on doing just that—living for the first time in over 40 years.

There are two phrases I use often.

"Only you can prevent forest fires."

And

"Not my monkey, not my circus."

They refer to different parts of similar scenarios.

“Only you can prevent forest fires” means only you are responsible for your life—only you!!! This is an incredibly important topic to me because I didn’t just lose years to this mindset—I lost decades. I sat in my victim story blaming everyone and everything for my own unhappiness. I gave myself every excuse under the sun for staying unhappy, too.

It was my ex’s fault. He was controlling and wouldn’t let me be me. Truth? No one can control you without your consent. I know that is a blunt statement and the reality is much more complicated —especially when emotional abuse is all you know. But finding out that I actually had power and could make choices for my own life changed everything.

I was a stay-at-home mom and hadn’t worked for years prior to becoming a yoga instructor, so it was easy to give myself the excuse that I couldn’t survive financially without my ex. I chose to stay in a place where I was broken and sad because I told myself I couldn’t be okay on my own.

I told myself that I was staying for my kids. In this world where very few people stay together, I wanted my kids to have Mom and Dad. Little did I realize that what my kids really needed to see was Mom standing up for herself, loving herself and having courage. Those things would have benefited them more than watching their parents continue to hurt each other.

“Only you can prevent forest fires” is an important statement to me because it reflects a deeper truth: only you can pursue your own happiness. Only you are responsible for your happiness. Only you can choose differently if you want happiness. And when I realized this truth, life changed.

I no longer lived in a victim story. I was able to own that if I wasn't happy, it was because the choices I made were not right for me. So I need to make different choices. The definition of insanity is to make the same choices and expect a different result. And yes, everything in your life reflects a choice you made. Take responsibility for your life. It is, after all, yours.

Leaving my marriage was terrifying, yet I did it anyway—and look at me now! I would never have been happy if I stayed. Frankly, I'm not sure I would still be alive. I was going down a pretty dark path.

But now, my life is filled with love. I have a career that I am passionate about and have found what matters to me. I will forever be thankful for whatever gave me the courage to change my life, despite my mountain of excuses.

Feel the fear and do it anyway. Believe me, because everything I ever wanted was just waiting for me on the other side of my excuses.

But the other phrase "not my monkey, not my circus" refers to dealing with people who are still where I used to be, stuck in their victim stories.

Those of us who have yet to see their own power and are trying to give you the responsibility of their happiness. They haven't yet learned that they are the only ones who can pursue their own happiness.

They will blame you, just like I blamed my ex and the world, for their misery and they will think you can save them. You can't. Don't take on their monkeys.

You can love them. You can listen to them. But you can't save them because they have to save themselves.

When people aren't well, they will use tactics to make you feel horrible that they are not okay. Things like guilt and manipulation.

They will attempt to make you feel like it's all your fault. But, my friend, it's not.

And until they have the courage to take control of their lives they will never be happy. So, if you continue to dance their dance, you are not helping them, you are hurting you.

Believe me, I've danced the dance my whole life. It hurts. Tears you up inside. Makes you lose yourself trying to save the people you love.

But instead you enable them to stay where they are, which is comfortable in their own misery.

If I can leave you with two things after all of this, it'd be the following: This is your life. YOURS. Don't give it away. Don't waste years forgetting how powerful you are. You can do hard things! I know change is scary, but if you want something different, you must do different.

Don't take on other people's pain. You cannot fix them, and you don't do yourself or anyone any favours by dancing an impossible dance. Love them and trust that they have the strength to find themselves.

And then, go find yourself.

After all, YOU have had the power all along.

Have you ever grieved over the past? I think it's something that we all face at some point. Life happens, and once things change, you can never go back. When you are younger, you don't think about it. You can't wait for time to pass. You don't realize that the moments in time you love will disappear and there will be no return.

I will never be a kid again, singing in the back seat of my parent's car with my sister. I will never go shopping with my mom. I will never hear her call me "Sherreeeey" or "Lovey"…

I will never hold my kids again like I did when they were little. I will never be able to keep them home from school so that we can have a day together. I will never sit in the living room with my kids and their dad, watching a movie. I will never wrap presents and hide them under the Christmas tree pretending to be Santa. I will never go for walks with them, singing.

I will never go back to my parents' house with both of them there, visiting and going to the mall together. I will never hear them bicker at one another, and my mom call my dad "Sugar Babe," and my dad call my mom "the Boss".

All of this is gone, and I will never be able to go back.

And I know that this is the nature of life. I know that even though those things are gone, I have new things to cherish now that I need to truly appreciate, because one day, these days will be gone too.

I have moments like last night when my youngest daughter stayed over and watched a scary movie with Dale and me. I have moments with Dale, cuddling on the couch and going on adventures together. I have moments watching him play with my dog, Beaker, who is getting older, and I know I need to cherish. I have moments teaching yoga.

I have so many beautiful things in my life right now.

But there is something so heartbreaking about losing the past and those beautiful memories that I'll never ever ever get to go back to.

I'm so grateful to remember.

It teaches you how special life is and how fleeting moments are.

And it makes time precious.

I don't want to waste any of it.

I woke up to a beautiful sunrise this morning.

Frankly, living in a high-rise apartment, I'm blessed with many beautiful sunrises. So many it's to the point now that I rarely stop to take a photo or even gaze at it. It becomes just another beautiful sky. I mean, I still notice it, but it's different. When I first moved into my apartment, I took pictures almost every morning, constantly admiring and in awe of the sky.

It's funny how the extraordinary can become ordinary.

I want to be mindful of that. I want to always be aware of the beauty around me. I don't want to take anything for granted.

Today would have been the 52nd birthday of a dear friend of mine. Her name was Rox-Ann and she was a firecracker of a woman. Small in stature but huge in personality. I met her in high school and we became fast friends.

Looking back, I can see how hurt she was. She lacked self-confidence and was what my mother would have termed "boy crazy". She made some mistakes that cost her some friends, but I was always there for her.

She moved first from my hometown. These were the days before social media and we lost contact. It would be many more years before we would find each other again.

By this time she had been through a lot. She had married and had a daughter, and then her husband passed away. She then remarried with two more sons.

During the time we reconnected, her second marriage had dissolved and her mental health declined. She ended up in a toxic relationship with someone who brought hard drugs into her life.

Ultimately the drugs took her.

I think of her often. During the years we were able to reconnect, she was so proud of me. I was beginning to model and she was my biggest fan. And even after her death, every once in a while, I open my Facebook to see a memory from her that feels like a reminder that she is still around me.

She was a beautiful woman and I'm sorry that her life was so short. She deserved more. Her kids did too.

She will never hug her kids again. She will never listen to a good song. Or eat a peanut butter sandwich. She will never dance again. Or brush her teeth. She won't get to do any of the ordinary things I get to do today. Let alone see the magnificent sunrise I got to see outside my window today.

Knowing this reminds me to not take anything for granted.

Especially that sunrise.

Magic happens every day, if you are paying attention.

I've been thinking about my mom a lot over the past few days. I've been going back over things I wrote a year ago when I was home visiting my dad and brother. That was the first trip home since mom passed and she was heavy in my mind. I wrote a lot about her.

I woke up yesterday and was scrolling through my phone, doing my morning routine, when I saw a post about grief and it made me cry. I haven't cried about my mom for a while. So when I went to work, she was still on my mind.

I was working the front desk at a gym, and almost as soon as I got there, a man came up to the counter asking for my manager. I told him no, but immediately we ended up in conversation.

He was an older man, 73 years old, and I remember his age because I filled out his information for a membership at the gym. He had a million stories to tell. He had been a musician. A drummer to be exact. He had these beautiful bright blue eyes and he was very charismatic. But you could tell he was lonely.

For two hours he talked to me. It was wonderful because my six-hour shift felt shortened by his company.

But what was so magical were the synchronicities between us. Both his parents were musicians and he spoke about the music that brought memories of his mom back to him. I can relate deeply to that. While my mom was never a professional singer, my own memories are filled with her singing, and there is so much music that always reminds me of her.

Eventually I would learn his mother was small in stature (only 5'1") and her name was Audrey and she had blue eyes. My own mom was even smaller (4'11") and her name was also Audrey and she also had blue eyes.

He was born in Nova Scotia just like my own parents, and when I told him where I was born, he told me that he had once visited my hometown to play music. He remembered the year, 1972. That was the year I was born.

The more we spoke, the more I was convinced he was an earth angel, sent to me by my mom to remind me she is still with me. Over our conversations, he asked me my name and I told him Sherr to which he replied, "just like Sunny and Cher." We talked a bit about Sunny and Cher and the old TV show that they used to have, and then quickly moved on to other topics.

But as he went to leave, two hours later, he announced that when he saw me next time, he would call me Sunny, not Sherr, because it suited me more, and began singing the same song my mom sang to me when I was small.

"You Are My Sunshine".

Every one of us has paranormal gifts. Did you know this? It's not limited to only certain people. It's all of us.

But not everyone believes, and if you don't, you will never see it. And like any skill, you must train yourself to be able to get better at it.

My mom was always connected to her gifts. She was deeply intuitive. But we were religious so that was unacceptable and not spoken of.

I only really started to believe and use my own gifts five years ago, when I had a spiritual awakening during the traumatic ending of my marriage. I have learned this is very common. Many people awaken after something brings their entire world down. Rock bottom often comes with the realization of something higher involved in our lives.

This was my experience.

Synchronicity started to follow me around. And music started to come with messages. I know that I've been sent songs at the exact time I needed the messages in their words. I started to use divination to help guide me, and started to collect oracle decks and tarot cards. I learned about crystal healing and have countless crystals all over my home. I did my three reiki attunements to become a reiki master. These seemed to crack me right open to my spiritual gifts.

I also had my first experiences with mediumship.

Yes, mediumship. It all started when I met someone who had tragically lost his past girlfriend due to kidney failure. Shortly after we met, I would repeatedly feel her presence around me. It was the strangest thing, and it would continue to happen for as long as he was in my life.

I was intrigued. I had never experienced this before and didn't even realize it was a gift of mine.

I wanted to pursue it so I took mediumship classes to try and grow the ability. When I performed reiki sessions on people, it would happen again.

Over the past five years, I have successfully communicated with many souls who are no longer here in human form. It's been a very cool experience, and definitely not something that I ever thought I could do.

The very amazing and exciting truth is that magic is indeed real, and we are not alone! When you are willing to see, you will find there is guidance everywhere. I personally believe in spirit guides and angels. I feel the presence of something around me.

But what solidifies my belief even deeper has been the passing of my own mom who had her own gifts when she was alive. Since she has left her physical form, I have had many experiences of her coming to me. I know she is still with me.

All of this has given me a sense of peace as well as the understanding there is nothing to fear.

I now believe that death is only just the beginning.

Something very magical happened during the visit I made last year to my parents' home. Mom had been gone for over a year then and I was there for what would have been my parents' 62nd wedding anniversary.

That morning I was getting ready to go with my brother to pick up my dad from the hospital to take him out for lunch. We had made the decision to not tell my dad it was his anniversary. The dementia would make him forget, and if we told him, we would also have to tell him Mom was dead. We didn't want to make him sad. We didn't want to make him relive that again.

So I was getting ready in my parents' bedroom and speaking aloud like she was there with me like I often do. I said to her "Mom, you are coming with us today" and as the words left my mouth, my eyes landed on a gold cross necklace hanging from the corner of the mirror above her dresser. I reached to pick up the necklace and felt another necklace hidden behind the mirror. As I pulled it out, I realized it was a small silver pendant with an angel carved on the front. As I turned the pendant over, I saw the words engraved.

ALWAYS WITH YOU

I know she is.

If there is a will, there is a way.

My mom used to say that, and that statement has gotten me through many things in my life. But sometimes it means stepping into fear. When I ended my marriage, I had never been alone. I had married him at the age of 19, and I had never lived alone. I leaned on him for protection. Leaving him meant leaving everything I knew. It meant stepping into the unknown. And I didn't have anything. My job didn't make enough to support my life. I couldn't afford a place on my own. I didn't know how I was going to do it.

But I had hit my rock bottom and there wasn't any other choice. It was stay and die, or take a leap of faith.

There was a moment where I believe something magical happened.

It happened during a text confrontation with my ex-husband. I already knew at the time I had to end the marriage. The only thing that was holding me back was overwhelming fear. My ex was bombarding me with messages, demanding to know if I was still willing to try and fix things. The months prior were filled with confrontation and I had felt manipulated and scared. Could I stand up to him? Could I face the mountain of fear in front of me?

I stared at the phone in front of me, frozen in terror.

And then it happened. On my phone popped up the image of a Goddess I already had tattooed on my skin. Kali Ma, the goddess of liberation from fear and ego.

These words accompanied that very picture:

KALI - Liberation

"You're being invited by the Hindu goddess of liberation and revolution, Kali, to address the aspects in your own shadow nature that have held you hostage to old ideas that no longer serve who you want to become. You can no longer define yourself by your victim story and expect to succeed in your life. There is a beauty in liberation that is deep, fierce, and courageous. It rises up from the willingness to break the chains of the past in order to transform into something new." - Colette Baron Reid

I still credit that specific moment as one of the most magical moments of my life. It literally felt like Kali herself had come to me in my most desperate moment.

Right then and there, I ended my marriage. Everything in my life changed.

And I learned something. Everything I ever wanted was on the other side of that damn fear.

Since ending my marriage, my whole life has changed and I've accomplished so many things I'm so proud of, and I've healed greatly from the broken woman who stared in terror at her phone that day.

I believe that great Goddess Kali came to me that day, and I believed she helped me. I'm forever grateful.

But today, I face new fears. Can I jump into the unknown again? Can I risk everything hoping that I'll be okay again? Is everything still waiting for me on the other side of my fear?

If there is a will, there is a way.

Watch me.

I'm different.

And yes, I do believe that we all feel like we are. We all feel weird or like we aren't like other people. I think that's a very human thing to feel.

But legitimately I've come to believe I'm different.

It would have been eight years ago now. The summer before I took my yoga teacher training. I was signed up and excited for where the path would take me.

One August day, I walked into a metaphysical store with my daughters and husband.

Back then, the contents of the store were intriguing yet foreign. Crystals, tools of divination, and books on witchcraft. Now, they are a part of my life like brushing my teeth, but back then, they were mysterious.

I had always wanted to be magical. Little did I know I already was.

I caught the eye of one of the people who worked there and was approached by him, asking if he could give me a reading. My answer was a resounding "Yes please". I always wanted to receive a reading from a psychic, and he was offering it for free.

Some of what he said still stays with me today.

He looked at the tattoo of my daughters as fairies on my left arm, and pointed to the one representing my oldest daughter. He said he saw her at my heart holding a book. From the time my daughter was old enough to hold a pen, she has been a writer. Looking back now, this also could have foretold my own journey to becoming an author.

He said I was Fae and asked me if I knew what that meant. I wasn't sure except that I know it's another way to speak of fairies, and I've always felt a connection to them. I have several fairy tattoos.

When I looked up the meaning of Fae, I found that they are less than Gods but more than mortal. They are known for their mischief and fiery nature.

But what he said last struck me hard.

He said I was to be the teacher of women.

Here I was less than a month from starting my journey to where I am now. And while I think I have taught many women the things I have learned, I know I've impacted many men as well.

He had no reason to know the journey that was coming.

Since that day, I've had several similar experiences with people randomly coming up to me and telling me interesting things.

Once, after leaving my ex and moving into my apartment, I was supplementing my income working for a beauty supply. There was a coffee shop next door and a man dropped his coffee in front of my store. He came in, asking for paper towels and ended up telling me something strange.

He told me I was a starseed. There is a belief that there are certain individuals born human but who actually are alien. They come here to help humanity. He believed I was one of them.

Later, I would find out this man was engaged to the woman who I took some of my first yoga classes with and who taught me the truth of yoga, and ultimately made me want to become a yoga teacher. Crazy world.

I don't believe in accidents.

Am I Fae? Or am I a starseed alien here to help humanity? I don't know about that. But I do feel I am different.

I see the world in a way few others do. I love hard. I'm not afraid of saying what I think, even if others may think I'm strange.

And I do believe my soul chose to come here to help others in pain.

I have a 13-year-old morkie named Beaker. He's been on this entire journey with me.

We brought him home when he was 8 weeks old to the day, on January 20th- my youngest daughter's 14th birthday.

In the past, my ex and I had trouble trying to be dog parents.

Our first dog, Kurgan, suffered from seizures and we struggled with trying to control them. We would put him on medication and the dosage would increase as the seizures kept happening. We tried. The seizures were devastating to witness. Eventually, he would pass away in our kitchen with me by his side. My husband was away on a business trip and it was mine to face alone.

Like many other things.

His short life was very difficult.

Our second dog, Bart, was a bull terrier who had aggressive tendencies from a puppy. He would get increasingly worse until I was terrified of him, and also terrified he'd hurt the kids, who at the time were still small. One night, while my ex was on another business trip, he bit my hand, ripping open my thumb.

We tried with multiple different trainers and experts but ultimately we were advised he was too dangerous, especially since I was afraid. Dogs smell fear, and no matter how hard I tried to pretend otherwise, he knew. And as long as he knew, he knew he was the boss of me. I couldn't control him.

So under the advice of the dog specialist we hired, we euthanized him.

It was my fault.

So when we brought home this tiny being that literally was small enough to fit in my hand, I was determined this time would be different.

He's my lucky puppy. I have him tattooed as a lucky cat (but in dog form) on my arm. We got him just as my oldest left for university.

I needed him more than I can express in words. I was lonely, sad, fighting with my youngest daughter and estranged from the man I slept beside. And my oldest daughter was leaving for university.

I was alone.

And he came.

Since that day, he's been by my side. I do believe that he has invisible wings. Through my hardest days, he's been here. My one constant.

Everyone left, but he stayed.

I love him more than words.

And now that Dale is in our life, Beaks has another person to love him. This makes me happy because Beaks deserves all the love in the world.

You get two choices in this life: get better or get bitter.

No one gets through life without experiencing pain. Every person who is reading this right now knows difficulties—betrayal, feeling abandoned, self-criticism. Many of us know trauma and abuse, all to different degrees. And some of us, unfortunately, know deep, horrible things.

But some of us don't even acknowledge our painful pasts. Pain is all we know. It feels normal.

It's like a setting on the dryer.

I think I lived like that most of my life. Sad was my normal. I knew nothing different.

It wasn't until I went on this journey to healing that I realized there was even a choice. I didn't have to stay in my pain. I could heal. I could face what hurt me and let it go.

As soon as I started to heal, I was grateful—and believe me, this hasn't been an easy path. I have had to face parts of myself that I wasn't proud of. I had to let go of my victim story that was making everyone else responsible for my unhappiness. Victim stories make us feel righteous in our anger, and it's easy to play the victim and make the world the villain. When you stop playing victim, you need to own your shit, and that's hard. Even painful. But! You also get to take your power back!

When you realize your happiness was never anyone else's responsibility, everything changes because now you need to be responsible. You need to change if you are not happy. You realize that this life is yours and you do get a choice. You are no victim.

And for me, my pain has now softened me. I want nothing more than to share my story so that others who are where I was, can choose to take their lives back too.

I'm not ashamed of my pain like I used to be. There is no more hiding. This is me. This is my story. And it's not a crazy outrageous story. It's a very normal story that so many of you out there understand. This is exactly why I share. Because so many of us are living in our pain like it's a setting on a dryer: normal.

But you don't have to. There's another way.

And I'm proof of that.

When people show you who they are, believe them.

I want to see the good side in everyone, and I believe we all have one.

This particular trait of mine has not always served me, it's made me ignore red flags regardless of if I could see them. I can also see their pain and the things they carry, and why they sometimes act in a way that is not kind, and I want to love everyone.

But when you disregard what people show you, two things happen:

You enable them to continue bad behaviour.

You abandon yourself because you give them the opportunity to do the same to you.

If someone steals and you witness it; they will steal from you.

If you see someone lie to another person; they will lie to you.

If someone talks poorly about someone to you; they will talk poorly about you to someone else.

If someone disregards others and doesn't care about hurting them; they will do the same to you.

People are rather simple creatures, and if you are observant, they will show you who they are. But whether you believe them when they show you, well, that's on you.

Having said that, other people's behaviour has nothing to do with you. It's not a personal attack. It's part of what they carry, and for many people, acting in these ways was what they learned to do to take care of themselves. Since they had life experience where no one else took care of them, they learned how to do it in ways that didn't care about hurting others.

No one cared for them. Why should they care for others?

And while I can definitely have sympathy for that, it's not my responsibility to fix broken people. It's my responsibility to take care of myself in the most loving way. I can't change someone else. I can only change me. So when I identify someone in my life who does not have my best interests in their agenda, it is my job to walk away or limit what contact they have with me.

And still send them love and healing.

From a distance.

You cannot heal in the same environment that made you sick.

This statement made me think about myself and my life, and about some of my loved ones and where they currently are.

I used to be really sick, but I thought it was normal. It was normal for me. It was what I grew up in. I didn't know any different. How can you possibly change what you don't know is wrong?

I did know I was unhappy. That I felt alone. That I lived in a certain amount of fear. That getting words out was difficult. And I did know that I should hide certain things from other people. I didn't want anyone to know about certain aspects of my life.

And from the outside, I think it looked like I had a blessed life. Even my parents and close friends didn't know, although I'm certain they had suspicions.

And there were no villains. Only people in pain who were like me. Sick but they didn't know it. Even that took me time to realize and to stop blaming others.

But luckily, getting better allows you to see things more clearly, and yes, I had to leave to get better.

The universe will force you to face your pain. If you choose to ignore it, the universe will turn up the volume on that pain until it's so severe you have no choice but to face it. That's what happened to me. The pain was so intense I didn't have a choice. There was no possible way I could've continued to stay where I was.

Rock bottom.

I now know that rock bottom is a powerful place to be because it is the beginning of what's next, and when we get there, there are two choices: get better or get bitter. I chose better. But not everyone chooses that. I can't control that. I can't fix others regardless of how deeply I want to.

So sometimes you must leave people you love because they won't choose to get better, and staying with them is making you stay sick.

And that breaks my heart. But it's true

I've been in deep self-reflection mode lately.

I know I still have room for growth, but I've noticed some shifts recently that have me seeing the change within myself.

I used to depend very heavily on the guidance of close friends. I shared everything with them. And then life evolved and they weren't there anymore. I went through grief and anger over that for a while.

I still miss them.

But I need to acknowledge that being on my own has actually been a benefit.

And it's not because my friends had any sort of bad intentions—they tried to help guide me, just like I've tried to help guide them.

But my friends don't live in my brain. They don't know what it's like to be me. I'm the only one who knows. And even with their best intentions, I know they caused me to overthink scenarios that I already knew the answers to. They prevented me from following my inner guidance. My intuition.

Being on my own forced me to trust myself more. And that has helped me stop overthinking the way I used to.

It's probably why I feel so at peace right now.

All the answers you seek are within.

Truly.

The dark goddess.

It is a topic I hear about often, especially in the spiritual community.

Medusa. Hecate. Lilith. Kali. Any goddess who has duality—darkness and light. Of the four I mentioned, three are tattooed on my skin.

They appear evil. Dark. But in reality, they represent strength. Standing up for oneself. Feminine power

Women who stand up for themselves often are judged. But women who behave well, hardly make history.

Behave well. What do those words actually mean to me?

My whole life, I've believed that I needed to be "good" to be loved. That included doing what I'm supposed to do. I can acknowledge my morality is high. I have a strong inner compass that guides me in what I believe to be right and wrong, and I do my best to adhere to it.

I work hard. I tell the truth. I stand up for what I believe in.

But a lesson I've also learned is that it's in our mistakes that we learn. I've been really messy. I've drank too much. I've dated multiple men. I've gossiped. I've reflected on my choices and realized I made poor decisions.

So what?

Old me would still be holding on to self-judgement and shame, but now I refuse to tear myself apart for something I can't change.

Did I make bad decisions? Yes. But those are the things that taught me what I want and what I don't want. I'm a better person because of those mistakes.

So I don't regret them. In fact, I actually credit them for helping build who I am today.

I grew up with a strict Christian father who taught me that I would go to hell if I made wrong choices. I grew up believing that I needed to be "good," and those beliefs caused me way more harm than any of the mistakes I've made.

I grew up with a mother who held deep shame about what it means to be a woman. You must be virtuous and innocent. Women did not explore their sexual nature. Women were to be pure. I've learned to embrace my feminine sexuality and realize there is nothing wrong or bad about it.

I no longer believe that God hates us and judges us when we lose our way. God is love. And God (or Goddess) above all, knows this is how we learn.

So perhaps I've learned to honour the dark feminine within me. Because it was in my darkness I found the light.

Introspective thoughts.

I felt overwhelmed today.

I've been running on next to no sleep, and I'm someone who needs her sleep. I've been working the 4am shift all week and still teaching my classes, as well as babysitting my daughter's pets while she is away on vacation.

Don't get me wrong, I'm grateful for it all. I love teaching my yoga classes. I am thankful to spend time with my grand-fur babies and I love them beyond words. And I'm so happy that my kids are able to go away and take some well-deserved time on their own. And I'm glad that they trust me with their precious babies.

The 4am shifts are also a gift because the hours will help me so much.

These are all wonderful things.

But I took on a lot today.

I made a list of things I needed to do: laundry, replacing the litters, taking garbage out, cleaning etc. Things I would need to do in the few hours between classes and work. I filled up my laundry bin to overflow and began to drag it down the hallway of my apartment building, heading to the laundry room. The heaviness was difficult to pull and the handle of my laundry bin broke off in my hand.

This is how I do things.

I don't ask for help. I pile up as much as I can and I push through until something breaks.

This has always been my way. Do not depend on anyone else. Never delegate. And then feel overwhelmed and resentful.

Strangely, I have taken pride in this trait. I spent years of my life alone taking care of the house and kids. If something needed getting done, I would find a way. I did it all alone.

The broken handle of my laundry bin is only one of the things I've broken trying to do too much.

But as much as I'm referring to material things breaking, I'm also thinking of myself. How hard can I push myself until I break?

Maybe it's okay to not have to do everything. And maybe pushing too hard until something breaks isn't a good thing.

I know I have deeper levels to heal. Being human means I will always be learning and growing. But I have to say, I feel really solid in where I am now.

Emotionally, I feel balanced. Of course my emotions fluctuate, especially with so much going on in my life and my dad having dementia. But there is no longer a war within myself. I allow myself to feel.

Yes I have things I know I could be better at. I still have some people-pleasing traits and there are times when I know I still have fear in speaking my truth, but I know exactly where I am and the things I could improve on. And I am not being self-critical, I am just aware. This thing called life is a journey, not a destination.

But mostly, and this is the biggest reason I feel so solid, I have faith.

I understand what we are and how we work. I have been learning about manifestation since my awakening five years ago, and it has taken me different levels to fully comprehend. And having the extra time lately to study the laws of the universe has benefited me greatly. I understand how every single thought, word, belief or action creates ripples into the world. And I can identify when something I did has made something specific come back to me.

It’s all really magical

We live in this beautiful, magical world, and the majority of us have no idea about our own power. How each of us can create ripples of positivity in the world and have it all returned to us.

And it’s been coming back to me. The more I give, the more I have. The more I stop controlling, the more everything flows easily. The more I have faith, the easier it all becomes.

It’s a wonderful place to be in.

What if it was all a gift? All of it?

Because I think it is. And I know that this triggers the hell out of some people who have had truly horrible experiences. How could the amount of suffering a person has had to endure be a gift?

Well, in my personal story, my trauma led me to what I do today. My pain brought me to my purpose. I do what I do today because of it.

It matters to me to help others in their pain because I know what it feels like. My passion comes from my personal experience.

And I look around me at the incredible people in this world and I see that some of the most remarkable people evolve from great pain.

In my personal life, I think of people like my friend Joelle, who overcame cancer, domestic violence, and a lifetime of self-loathing. My friend Ashley, who overcame a life of sex work, a life-threatening fall while working construction (which she now credits with changing her life), and a lifetime of self-hatred. My friend Sasha, who overcame drug abuse and violence, as well as self-esteem issues.

Because they have endured pain, they prioritize kindness and want to make a difference.

There is a particular famous person who I often quote during my classes. Her name was Maya Angelou, and her life was filled with pain. She was raped as a young child by her uncle, and once she told someone what had happened, he was murdered. She blamed herself for his death and believed her voice had the power to kill. So she stopped speaking. For years.

But with the encouragement and constant love of her grandmother, she would eventually speak again, and her words still ripple into the world today. She became a highly renowned poet, author, and activist who had a difficult yet fascinating life. Her wisdom still inspires me, which is why I constantly use her words in my classes.

"Do the best you can until you know better. Then when you know better, do better."

"When someone shows you who they are, believe them the first time."

"You teach people how to treat you."

And of course, "There is no greater agony than bearing an untold story inside you."

To me, she represents the wisdom that can come from pain. Pain is a remarkable teacher, if you are willing to forgive the past and see it differently.

My past experiences have taught me so much, and they led me to the life I now have. I get to help others and I am beyond grateful for it all. To me, every single day I am thankful that this is my path.

I will continue to share my journey and do my best to make a difference. And I will continue to tell my story, in hopes someone out there needs to hear it.

You can't make your life decisions based on what people think.

You can't, because if you do, you will miss out on experiencing the most beautiful things.

I clearly don't live my life worrying about what others think, but my parents sure did. It used to really bother me. Someone from the church would make a surprise visit to the house and they'd be running around hiding the evidence that they smoked cigarettes.

My mom really cared. She grew up hearing people gossip about her mom. My grandmother had a reputation for being a "whore," and in the small town in Nova Scotia that my mom grew up in, people talked.

It left a mark on my mom. It formed how she raised her kids. It left a mark on me.

Women had to be modest and pure.

But women are sexual beings, just like men, and this world has made that wrong, creating so much harm. I myself have had to reflect on and face the beliefs my mother instilled in me that made me feel shameful about my own sexuality.

However, a big aspect of my personality is rebelliousness, and I honestly think that watching my parents worry so much about other people's opinions made me who I am.

Hence the tattoos and piercings. I was not like the other moms picking up their kids at school.

When my marriage ended, there were no longer any restrictions on me and I could be myself completely. This revelation resulted in way more tattoos (my goal is a full body suit someday), more piercings and wild, colourful hair.

It's my personality too. I say what I think. There isn't much of a façade going on with me. And I'm pretty sure some of my beliefs cause some others to think I'm weird. And that's okay! I'm here to make you think. And to pull down the curtain that we've all been hiding behind.

For the right people, I will help them be themselves.

I believe we need to come back to who we were before the world told us there was something wrong with us.

But it's also in my life choices. Dale is 20 years younger than I. My family wasn't surprised by my choice, but his family was. And I know not everyone will agree with us.

But that's okay.

You can't make your life decisions based on what others think. If I had, I would have missed out on Dale. And he's incredible.

Someone asked me why so many people are afraid to speak up or be different.

What came to me is this:

Most people don't even like themselves. Self-worth and self-confidence and self-love are things most of us struggle with.

So if you don't even like yourself, how can you possibly feel confident about your opinions, or even who you are?

And if you are always putting yourself down, wouldn't you expect others to do the same?

I know how it feels to be that person with that voice in my head telling me how stupid I am. I know how it feels to feel like you don't fit in. I know what it feels like to want to be liked.

Many of us will hide ourselves and try to morph into what we believe others want, instead of being authentic.

We all just want to be loved.

In Canada, faith is a very personal thing and most of us avoid speaking about our personal beliefs to others. Myself included. I grew up with Christianity thrown at me. You must believe or you will spend eternity burning in hell. As a child, this terrified me. As I grew older, this baffled me. I had questions but I wasn't supposed to ask them. I was supposed to blindly accept things. Well, I couldn't do that. So as an adult, I stepped away from Christianity.

My children were not raised in religion, but we still talked about faith. I told them my beliefs. I told them I believed in a higher power, but not necessarily religion. I told them I struggled with any religion that created separation or judgement.

When I had my "awakening" something shifted. Faith became undeniable. Without any doubt I knew that there was something guiding me. Without doubt I knew I was not alone.

My yoga classes are very much an expression of me. I don't just guide people into yoga poses—I storytell through the class and I teach about the chakras. Sometimes I tell my class things I've gone through.

But at first, I was nervous to speak about faith.

It's important to me to hold space for other people's beliefs. I never want them to feel like I am forcing my beliefs on others. I think this stems back to how I felt about my own religion as a child. So I held back.

Lately, I haven't been holding back. I've been sharing my personal beliefs always with the disclaimer that I'm not trying to convert anyone, and that if the practitioner has their own beliefs, they are welcome to incorporate them into the class.

There is a part of me that still worries about how the people in my class are going to react. Are they uncomfortable with me talking about faith? Do I offend?

But I also believe in being fully authentic, which means I don't hide any aspect of who I am, and my faith is a huge part of who I am. For me, faith has been a huge factor in my personal healing. My faith has carried me through many difficult times. My faith allowed me to face the pandemic without fear and to stand by the decision to not be vaccinated even though it meant facing a very unknown future. My faith allowed me to accept my mom's passing and to believe she is still with me. And my faith continues to give me hope for people in my life who are struggling. My faith has given me the strength to face fear. And my faith gives me the gift of hope.

And hope changes everything.

Hope gives us the willingness to look for the light even in the darkest of days.

So I think it is okay to talk about faith. My beliefs hold space for all religions. I refuse to believe that God hates someone because they call him a different name.

God(dess) is love after all.

My life is changing, and old things are falling away.

It's bittersweet.

There are parts of my past I miss. People I love who aren't around anymore. People who were important to my journey and to why I'm the woman I am today.

But I'm not on the same path with them anymore.

I won't lie, some of it's painful. And it's a lesson in understanding that staying in your own truth is important, and that it's not rejection. You can still love someone and know you are not aligned with them anymore.

But some of it's beautiful. I'm in a wonderful place. I have this amazing man in my life. And many other good wonderful friends. And I truly feel blessed.

I have released many negative things from my life that really don't serve me anymore.

And when I look in the mirror I see a woman who has overcome so much.

I'm truly and honestly proud of her.

Boundaries.

Five years ago I didn't understand what they were. Honestly, in some ways, I think I am still figuring it out.

Because it's more than expressing your emotions—it's expressing how you feel, and giving a consequence for the scenario happening again. And then holding true to that consequence.

Let me give you an example:

Saying "I feel like my time is disregarded when you are late" is stating an emotion.

Saying "I feel like my time is disregarded when you are late, and if it happens again, I will leave without you" is a boundary.

Stating the emotion used to be difficult in my past. Now I can do it easily. But setting the consequence and then implementing it is still a challenge.

I come from a lifetime of putting myself last and setting a consequence still feels like me being an imposition. Or being unkind. Who am I to tell someone what to do?

But the truth is that it's up to me to teach others how I want to be treated.

Logical me knows that it's my job to communicate my needs. Other people are not mind readers, and if someone is acting in a way that's hurtful to you and you don't tell them, you are not being fair to them either. You are not giving them the opportunity to fix the situation.

But after a lifetime of not wanting to impose on anyone, I'm still learning how to put myself first.

And it's a journey, not a destination.

Have you ever tried to use the laws of attraction in your favour? I have. Multiple times. And I know it to be real.

The laws of attraction state that whatever you focus on, you draw towards you. Simple and as complicated as that. And many people believe they can wield that understanding to create what they want in life. It's what we call manifestation, and while we all manifest, not all of us know that we are doing it. But many of us attempt to learn how to use our power to our advantage.

I personally have been pretty successful here.

One time I made a Facebook status putting out into the universe my intention to have a light coloured fur coat. Fur coats started randomly coming my way. Eventually after receiving six fur coats, I started having to turn them away.

I've manifested the apartment I live in. Five years ago, I pointed up near the top of the building and announced I would be living there. I was off by one apartment.

I started to model almost 20 years ago now, and in the beginning my goal was to be published in magazines. I was incredibly successful at this. I've lost count of my publications, and even magazine spotlights. But what I dreamed of most was seeing myself on the cover of a magazine. I pursued this hard, but it remained elusive.

Years later, I turned my attention towards my yoga instructor career and let go of the pursuit of my modelling career. I still continued to model but only for the fun of it. Modelling has always been a source of creativity for me and I have some wonderful friends because of it. I stopped pursuing publications completely, but I still would have loved to be on a magazine cover. I just stopped chasing it.

Since I released the need to control outcomes, my magazine cover just came to me. One day I opened my messages to a message from a magazine editor offering me the opportunity to be on the cover of their magazine. At the age of 49, I got my cover.

My books, including the one I'm writing now, are full manifestations. I always wanted to write and be published, and both opportunities found me from just that desire. No pursuit or chasing was involved.

And this is the key, because what you chase, you push away. The understanding is that if you are pursuing something with intensity, you must somehow not believe it could happen. And in manifestation, one of the key components is the belief that you can achieve.

What you think, you create.

This proved to be a difficulty for me when I was pursuing love. I wanted it too much. It was my greatest desire and I was, deep down, afraid I wouldn't find it. The harder I pursued, the more it remained elusive.

It took me getting hurt enough times, and getting to the point that I would rather be alone than with someone who wasn't right, to change my life. I stopped chasing love, and shortly after, Dale came into the picture.

He is my greatest manifestation.

But there still remains one more desire that continues to remain unfulfilled in my life. Stability. Money. Financial success. I understand that it's my deep desire and fear of not having enough that continues to keep me from manifesting it in my life.

But I'm working on it. And I know it's coming. Look at my life so far, I think I'm pretty good at the laws of attraction.

Without doubt it's coming.

I'm grateful.

What you think, you create. Think yourself unlucky and create bad fortune. But believe yourself blessed and create blessings.

So many of us walk this earth completely unaware of our own power.

I was the spoiled child. I am five years younger than my sister. I am the baby of the family. So my parents had a little more for me. A little more of everything. My mom said she had more patience with me than my siblings. And if I wanted something, I always got it.

My parents weren't wealthy, but I was never without.

Looking back, I understand that this was a very important blessing for me. From early on, I learned a lesson. I learned that I could get what I wanted.

So I took that belief and created a life that was different than others.

While my life hasn't been perfect, I've had many blessings.

I've experienced living in different parts of Canada. Many of the people I grew up with never left our home town.

I've been to Disney World four times, and Disneyland once. Many people only dream about going.

In my 30's, I began to model despite my age and unlikely appearance. I've been published multiple times and achieved a magazine cover only a couple years ago, in my late 40's.

My TikTok blew up with very little effort. I didn't pursue it. It just happened.

And I'm writing my second book.

I know that I'm rare.

And it's not that I'm any different than anyone else, but I do have something not everyone has.

The belief that I can.

And so I do.

You cannot give away what you don't have

You can only give away what you have inside.

This is why hurt people hurt others. If you are filled with anger and resentment and hatred and judgement, these will be your gifts to others.

But what you have inside is a reflection of what is on the outside. So when you fill yourself with love, love will appear around you.

You attract what you are.

If you want love, love others.

If you want others to be generous with you, be generous with others.

If you want to be understood, seek to understand.

“She wanted to change the world, so she started with herself.”

When you finally get clarity and you decide for the final time what you are willing to accept, it will surprise you how quickly the universe will conspire in your favour.

In Christian faith, they speak of “free will.” It’s why we can sin. God lets us choose.

Which, in hindsight, makes me wonder why we worry so much about doing things wrong. God gave us the ability to fuck up, and I have to think he did it for a good reason: so we can learn.

My fuck-ups have taught me everything I know.

They helped me understand, with clarity, what I want and do not want.

And I was brave enough to face my fears and jump into the unknown, I was rewarded with the life I have now. I just had to get clear about what I was willing to accept.

How beautiful?

As I am writing this, it's been a year today since I became a published author. Since my first book, *Good Morning*, entered the world.

It's bittersweet.

I mean, it's amazing. A literal dream come true. And I'm currently working on my second book. I'm beyond grateful, and I know that all of this has been divine. I manifested all of it.

From the time I was a little girl, I loved to write. But I never thought I could, so I left it alone. I let it go and didn't focus on it.

Two years ago it came to me.

I had been writing every single day, but not with any intention of becoming an author. I had just been writing to release my thoughts from my brain, so I took my thoughts and shared them on my Facebook. People started paying attention and I had many friends reach out to me to say thank you, and that something I wrote had resonated with them.

One of those friends happened to own her own publishing company and she asked me if she could put my thoughts into a book.

The rest is history.

So when people come to me for advice on how they, too, can get their book published, I don't really have an answer.

Write until someone notices?

I believe my writing was meant to be, even when I didn't know it, and I dream of my words travelling the world and helping people.

My oldest daughter also writes.

From the time she was able to put pen to paper she was making books. The early ones were stapled pieces of paper complete with drawings. I think I still have some of them stored away in remembrance of her childhood.

It's all she ever wanted, and I did my best to support her dream. I believe she was meant to write. It's a God-given gift.

A lot of people told her she could not.

A lot of people told her that becoming a successful published author was too difficult, and to give up and get a real job. Even her high school English teacher told her it wasn't possible.

But she didn't give up, and I supported her. I believed in her.

After high school, she went to university to receive her bachelor's degree in English. She followed that with her master's degree. She did well. My daughter is very intelligent.

And she never stopped writing. All she learned about getting published was that she needed to find an agent, who would, in turn, find her a publisher—that would be the best route for success. So she sent off her manuscript to many agents and received multiple rejections.

I tried to keep her hopes up. After all, when you look at the stories of some of the most successful authors, like Stephen King and J.K. Rowling, you find out that they, too, were rejected. And look at them now.

After I ended my marriage with her dad, we lived together for a short time period and we did not get along. When she left, our relationship changed and I no longer see her often. It's almost been a year now since I last saw her.

I miss her.

But I also can't help but feel strange about my own success with writing. After all, I watched my daughter try and receive rejection. I didn't even try and it came to me.

And I know that this is how manifestation truly works. What you cling to, you ultimately push away. The universe plays a cruel joke on us all. Don't want what you want too much or you will never get it.

I never even thought I could become an author, but I've always loved to write. Because I had no attachment to the result, it all just came to me. Literal manifestation. Literal magic.

So when these beautiful opportunities come to me, I think about her. And since I don't have her in my life right now, all I can do is send her my love from afar in hope that my luck rubs off on her.

And that her dreams come true too.

Yoga saved me. Yoga has transformed my life over and over and over again.

Funny thing was, I went to my first class because I thought I was going to exercise.

That is what Western culture thinks yoga is—just some stretching. That's the smallest part of yoga.

Yoga is literally thousands of years old, and its original purpose was to be medicine. Yoga is healing. It's not just physical healing, but also mental and spiritual. Yoga fixes everything.

If you have headaches or a bad back, do yoga. If you can't fall asleep, do yoga. If you are depressed, do yoga. If you feel alone, do yoga!!!

What you seek from yoga, you will find. But when I did my first class, I found the physical aspect and immediately fell in love. It felt so good!

It took a few years and the right teacher to realize that there was more to yoga than the strength and physical side.

One fateful day, I walked into a little apartment-turned-yoga studio, and it changed my life.

I can still smell the cinnamon tea as you walk in. Ganga always had tea steeping on the stove and snacks waiting on the table. As soon as you entered, you were in her kitchen, and to the front of the kitchen was her living room. She had no furniture. It was an open room so she could teach her classes there. I would frequent the classes as much as I could.

That little apartment would change what I thought yoga was. I was struggling at the time. When I look back, it feels like I was always going through something. But this was a particularly dark time in my life, and I truly think it was something divine that guided me there.

I needed help, and there it was in the form of an earth angel. Her name was Ganga. She embodied love and acceptance and she taught me the real meaning of yoga. It is she whom I credit as the reason why I now teach—because of what she gave me, I wanted to pass it on.

It would take me a while to figure out life enough to take the training and become a teacher, but doing so would also transform me in ways I couldn't have fathomed.

Teaching saved me. And I mean that.

By the time I took my training, life had continued to unravel in a very unhealthy way and I had no confidence or self-worth. In fact, I had no voice at all.

But yoga forced me to find my voice. Yoga pushed me out of my comfort zone and made me do things that helped me see my own inner strength.

Yoga helped me make connections with other people.

Yoga made me realize I wasn't alone.

And most of all, yoga showed me I was capable of doing hard things.

I actually believe I left my marriage because yoga gave me the strength to do it.

As I grew more confident as a teacher, I started to form my classes around the seven chakras. Once I started to teach the energy side of yoga, things really shifted. My classes became more than exercise. They became self-awareness work. And the benefits weren't only for those who came to my classes, but also for me.

While I was teaching, I was also learning.

And EVERYTHING shifted then.

I believe that yoga is actually a remembering of who you were, before the world told you it was wrong. It's entirely about coming back to the truth.

The word "yoga" translates into the word "union," and it reminds us that we belong to one another.

To me, yoga means love. And to this very day, it still saves me.

It says in the Bible 365 times that there is nothing to fear. One time for every single day of the year. And if you do truly believe in a higher power, then you know the good guys win.

When you can fully let go of fear and surrender, then you are finally free.

And I don't think it is about achieving a perfect life. It's about learning to live in peace, even within chaos.

It's strange, but I feel like I'm there right now.

As I was teaching last night, it hit me how much I have going on in my life right now.

I haven't seen my oldest in almost a year, and I think of her every day and pray she is okay.

My dad is still fading away in a long-term care facility, and every time I talk to my brother, I hear his struggles. I doubt my dad remembers me anymore.

My sister reached out a couple days ago with some health concerns and she's waiting to hear if she's okay.

I lost a close friend last week due to a disagreement where I feel she attacked me, accusing me of things that were unfair. I also think her mental health is not good, and despite the disagreement, I am worried about her.

If I were to lose myself even in one of these situations, I could take myself down a dark path. But I'm not. The world around me is in chaos and I am okay.

I am at peace.

I'm not assuming that I will always be at peace. I've come to realize that life is that ebb and flow. At some point, I'm sure I'll face grief, anger, fear and sadness again. Things are coming. But I've also come to experience deep faith over it all, and I know when (not if) they come, I will face them.

Focus on what you can control and let go of everything else.

Let go and let God.

So I'm choosing to focus on the things I have that are wonderful.

I have this book that I am writing and feeling very good about. I have Dale sleeping beside me. He truly gives me so much peace. I have my youngest daughter visiting us and I feel so grateful for the relationship we have now. I have my yoga class I'm teaching today and the wonderful people who are coming to it. There is sunlight coming through my bedroom window, and my dog Beaker is sleeping with us.

My life is filled with good things.

And at the very same time, there are things to worry about. But all of those things are out of my control. So I send my oldest daughter, my dad, my sister, my brother, and anyone else in my life who is struggling, my love. I wrap them in it. And I pray to God to keep them safe and lead them through their struggles.

"Everything will be okay in the end. If it's not okay, it's not the end." ~John Lennon

Most of my life I have felt unimportant. Invisible. Unwanted.

When I started teaching yoga and my teaching evolved into something more than just moving your body, but also learning about yourself, people started to tell me I was helping them.

Every single time I would hear that, it would be hard for me to receive. That I made a difference. That my voice—my words—could impact another in a meaningful way.

When I got home today, I received a message from someone somewhere out in this world who bought my book and is reading my words.

Still trying to let it sink in.

I make a difference. Me being here helps others. That is truly the most beautiful feeling.

Whatever you focus on grows.

If you are focused on how little money you have and the fear of not having enough, you will continue to lack abundance.

If you focus on how unwell you are, you will continue to get sick.

If you focus on how lonely you are, you will constantly find yourself alone.

But if you focus on gratitude and have faith that you can achieve, you will build financial success.

If you focus on your body's strength and resilience, you will become healthier.

And if you focus on the people you are blessed to have and all the love in your life, you will attract more people towards yourself.

Get clear what you are giving your energy to.

Things I have learned so far:

Don't worry about other people's opinions about you. After all, their opinions about you have nothing to do with you and everything to do with them. Their personal experiences and traumas and beliefs.

Follow your heart—it knows the way. And don't be so quick to question your own wisdom.

You won't find answers in other people. They are not on your path, they are on their own path, and their answers are not your answers. So as well meaning as people can be, when you start looking for answers in other people, you will be pulled from your own alignment. If you want to know the right way to go, look in the mirror, not to other people.

Your personal peace is the most precious thing you own, so the cost of losing it should reflect that. Don't give away your peace to something that won't matter tomorrow. Be very discerning about who gets to take it from you.

Everyone you meet has been through something. Be aware when you meet anyone and just be kind. There are so many of us that just need to feel seen. So when you meet someone, see them. Respect people. And do your best to always leave a positive impression on everyone you meet.

It's okay to put yourself first. In fact, it's important. It's the only way to build healthy relationships. Your job is to advocate for yourself, and other people's job is to advocate for themselves. When two people communicate their needs to one another, they become responsible to one another. They both are teaching each other how each other wants to be loved. No one feels put last or ignored. But it all starts with you taking care of you.

If you want to change the world, it starts in the mirror. Simple and as complicated as that. Because the ripple effect is real, and when you heal you, you impact everyone. Energetically, you shift your vibration, which has an impact on the energy you give out to everyone you meet. Logically, when you heal you, you learn communication, and this automatically impacts your relationships. And since humans are so interwoven and have such an ability to change one another, this will shift those close to you, and then they will shift those close to them, and so on. But if you seriously want to help the world, then start with yourself.

What you give returns to you. Want to be heard? Then listen. Want to be understood? Then seek to understand others. Want to be loved? Then love—unconditionally. Without expectation. And watch it all return to you. Maybe not in the way you think it should —but guaranteed what you give out to the world, you will get it back.

And that also includes the bad stuff. If you judge, you will be judged. If you hate, you will be hated. If you cheat, you will be cheated. What goes around comes around. So be mindful!

Every single day is a new one. Did you fuck up yesterday? Oh well, you now have today. And when you know better, do better.

So let's go do better.

My Dale asked me yesterday if I could have imagined where we are now. My answer was an absolute no.

Honestly, I could never have dreamed I'd be here. None of it. Working on my second book, on my second year with Dale, on my 8th year teaching, and my life filled with love. Grounded. Happy. Healthy physically, emotionally, and mentally.

And still healing, but so many miles away from the girl I used to be.

It's all a dream. An amazing, wonderful dream.

I woke up to see a quote from Joss Whedon that I had shared 12 years ago. Back then I certainly had no idea where life was going to take me but I had some really big moments coming that were going to change everything.

Despite being really hard, I'm so thankful for those moments because they lead me here.

"Bottom line is, even if you see them coming, you're not ready for the big moments. No one asks for their life to change, not really. But it does. So, what are we, helpless? Puppets? Nah. The big moments are going to come, you can't help that. It's what you do afterwards that count. That's when you find out who you are."
-Joss Whedon.

The sky is a reminder for me this morning.

Yesterday was cold. After a mild couple of months, the weather turned yesterday. All day long you could hear the wind howling. When I went out to teach classes or to run errands, I ran as quickly as I could to avoid spending time outside.

I can still hear the wind this morning.

But the sky is on fire. As cold as it is outside right now, the sky is red. As the sun rises, it's filling the skies with streams of red and orange. It's magnificent.

I've been teaching the third chakra this week: solar plexus. Your inner fire. Your ability to stand up for yourself, your purpose, boundaries, and your ability to be real and authentic.

In a world where people tell you what to be and what you can and can't do, it's remembering who you are.

Personal power.

Yesterday morning was stressful and it impacted the whole day. I found myself feeling exhausted, I couldn't even write last night after my classes. And I always love to write.

But all week, in my classes, I've been reminding people who they are. I make them rub their hands together and feel the warmth build between them.

We are made of Mother Earth. All five elements lie within us. Water. Earth. Air. Space. And… FIRE.

So on the very coldest day, remember who you are. Remember that fire lives within you, literally at your fingertips.

And that even when the world is raging and the wind howling, you will rise… again.

And light up the whole damn sky.

Sometimes life evolves in unexpected ways and takes you places you never imagined.

There was a time I believed my destiny was to be a mom to my girls and wife to my husband, and I wanted nothing more. I thought those were my most important roles.

Then my kids grew up and my marriage ended, and a whole new world that I never imagined came to me. It all started when I became a yoga teacher, and through that I was opened up to people and the realization that I could make a difference. I found my purpose. My reason for existence. I'm meant to help people.

And that single realization has brought me endless opportunities. But out of every beautiful thing that I never knew I'd get to do, my book is still my favourite. I'm a published author. I'm a published author. I'm a published author!!!!

And now there is this book: book number two! This is a dream come true...AGAIN! The dream that started as a little girl who loved to storytell but never believed she could. But I did! And I am! In the most rewarding way I could ever imagine. I get to help people find their way out of the darkness.

Author Brene Brown once said,

"One day you will tell your story of how you overcame what you went through and it will be someone else's survival guide."

Maybe someday someone will quote my words just like I did for Brene Brown. Maybe my words could inspire someone else. How wild would that be?

Brene Brown, Maya Angelou, Wayne Dyer, Joe Dispenza, Neal Donald Walsh, Ram Dass and so so so many other writers have helped me with their words of wisdom.

So I share with you my life in hopes that I may inspire you to also chase your dreams….

Because dreams do come true—I am proof.

One Day

One day you will see it was all a gift.

The pain.

The mistakes.

The wrong turns.

It was just leading you home.

Manufactured by Amazon.ca
Acheson, AB

15898928R00109